Situational Crime P
From Theory Into F

Edited by Kevin Heal and Gloria Laycock

HOME OFFICE RESEARCH AND PLANNING UNIT

LONDON: HER MAJESTY'S STATIONERY OFFICE

ISBN 011 340826 9

Contents

Foreword

The case for devoting more resources and research to the protection of people and property against robbery, burglary, theft and vandalism rests not merely on pessimism or scruples: pessimism about the efficacy of deterrence and correction, scruples about putting offenders out of action for long periods. Even if those strategies were more effective than they seem to be, a preventive policy would still make sense. We are no longer under the illusion that property offences are the work of a small minority of the population, or that the minority will be identified sooner or later in their careers. The potential offenders are numerous and by no means always recognisable. By contrast, we do at least know what property we want to protect, and where it is. And as the chapters in this collection demonstrate, we have good evidence that some techniques for defending it are fairly effective.

As the articles also show, however, crime prevention – like other policies – has to solve problems which are not merely technical. It has to convince the designers of buildings, the planners of urban environments, the organisers of communal vigilance that expert advice should not be ignored. Most difficult of all, perhaps, it has to persuade members of the public who are not architects, planners or vigilantes that they should not rely solely on law enforcement to provide the degree of protection which they demand. Propaganda seems to be making an impression, but more than that may be needed. As the Hodgson Committee pointed out – though it hardly needed pointing out – there are people who cannot afford insurance against theft or vandalism and there are also people who cannot spare money on self-protection. The State cannot, for the forseeable future, afford to compensate the uninsured against property offences; but it may be in the long run more effective to assist them to take preventive measures.

However that may be, we need thoughtful and critical arrticles of the kind which the editors of this volume have taken the trouble to assemble. They show us not only what is likely to work but also what is not. Fortunately most of what they tell us is encouraging. I hope we shall see more publications of this high professional quality.

NIGEL WALKER
King's College
Cambridge

June 1986

v

Editors' note

The chapters of this book fall into three parts. In the first (chapters 1 and 2), some of the theoretical ideas behind situational crime prevention are discussed. Chapter 1, by Derek Cornish and Ronald Clarke, concentrates upon the possibility of the displacement of crime and considers situational prevention within the framework of rational choice. The second chapter, by Gordon Trasler, is in some respects a critical commentary on the first; it raises a number of issues any developing theory attempting to explain criminal behaviour must take into account.

The second, and most substantial part of the book, considers the prevention of crime in a number of practical settings. Chapter 3, by Barry Poyner, provides a general introduction to this section in suggesting a model for action while the following chapters describe the outcome of the analysis of crime or the introduction of situational measures from a preventive perspective.

The authors of chapters 8, 9, 10 and 11, drawing on work from the United States, Canada, Sweden and the United Kingdom respectively, consider some of the practical issues arising from situational crime preventive activity in their countries. They are not theoretical in the sense of the first two chapters and will be of greater interest to the administrator or policy maker than to the academic.

All the work has been newly commissioned although some draws on earlier published material. The contributors come from the Home Office Crime Prevention Unit and Research and Planning Unit or are academics or practitioners from the United Kingdom and abroad.

KEVIN HEAL
GLORIA LAYCOCK
Queen Anne's Gate
London

June 1986

1 Situational prevention, displacement of crime and rational choice theory

Derek B. Cornish and Ronald V. Clarke

Traditional criminological perspectives have tended to be somewhat critical of the ideas underlying situational crime prevention. In their view, reducing opportunities for crime through environmental manipulation, while perhaps achieving limited and situation-specific decreases, would fail to lower crime rates overall. Instead, such measures would usually be thought to result not in the prevention of offending, but merely in its 'displacement' to some other time or place or, alternatively, to some other form of crime (cf. Reppetto, 1976; Gabor, 1978, for discussions of the concept of displacement). For reasons which we will examine later, belief in the inevitability of displacement continues to underpin much lay and professional thinking concerning the practicability of crime prevention policies and practices.

In the following discussion we look at the empirical evidence for displacement effects. Then, after briefly criticising the assumptions about criminal behaviour which tend to be encouraged by use of the term 'displacement', we go on to suggest that the phenomenon is better conceptualised in terms of a rational choice theory of criminal behaviour which views the bulk of offending as the outcome of largely reasoned decisions about the costs and benefits involved. After elaborating a series of models of offending behaviour within such a decision making framework, we conclude by discussing the implications of this perspective for the concept of displacement.

Empirical evidence relating to displacement

Despite the frequency with which the displacement hypothesis is offered as a crucial objection to situational crime prevention approaches, little systematic evidence about the phenomenon exists. In consequence, judgements about its likely importance can at present be formed only on the basis of a rather unsatisfactory amalgam of disparate findings. To begin with, there are some scattered examples of situational measures apparently achieving substantial reductions in specific forms of crime. Airliner hijackings which reached an annual average of about seventy in the early 1970s were reduced to about fifteen per year by the latter part of the decade through defensive measures taken by airlines and governments (Wilkinson, 1977). Cheque frauds in Sweden were greatly reduced in 1975 following the introduction of cheque guarantee cards (Knutsson & Kulhorn, 1981). An epidemic of thefts from a new kind of public telephone in Great Britain was eliminated by the wholesale replacement of aluminium by steel coin boxes (Mayhew *et al.*, 1976). And a law introduced in Great Britain in 1970 compelling motorcyclists to wear protective helmets had the unintended effect of greatly reducing motor-cycle thefts – presumably because the requirement to wear a helmet ruled out most spur-of-the-moment offences (Mayhew *et al.*, 1976). (Similar results have since been reported in other countries following similar legislation.) Perhaps the most impressive example, however, comes from West Germany where a 60% reduction in the rate of car thefts followed the compulsory introduction in 1963 of steering-column locks for all vehicles (Mayhew, *et al.*, 1976).

In all these various examples, significant and lasting reductions in specific forms of crime were obtained – evidence that situational measures do not always displace crime to some other time or place, or result merely in the modification of the methods by which these crimes are committed. But the record of situational measures is not one of unqualified success, and there are many examples of such measures which have, in fact, merely displaced the attention of offenders to some other target. For instance, the introduction in Great Britain of steering-column locks only for *new* cars resulted not in the overall reduction of vehicle theft but merely in its displacement from new to old cars (Mayhew *et al.*, 1976). Again, Chaiken *et al.* (1974) report that a police "crackdown" on subway robberies in New York City resulted in an increase of street robberies, while Allatt (1984) found that a burglary prevention exercise involving target hardening of an entire public housing estate in Newcastle displaced some burglaries to other houses nearby. Lastly, even where there is no evidence of these forms of displacement, the possibility cannot be ruled out that another form of displacement might have occurred namely, that the offenders concerned might have turned their attention to some other form of crime.

Assumptions underlying the displacement concept

Tentative and anecdotal though much of the evidence for displacement undoubtedly is, the concept both alerts the policy maker to the possibility that a range of unanticipated consequences may attend novel (or ill-considered) crime control policies, and suggests the various forms which these problems might take. But if such outcomes are to be averted, a clear and accurate understanding must also be gained of the mechanisms which give rise to them. And in this context, it is apparent that use of the term displacement to describe these possible consequences involves certain theoretical assumptions regarding the mechanisms likely to be implicated.

The term displacement has its conceptual roots in drive theories of motivation such as those of Freud (1940), Lorenz (1966) and Dollard and Miller (Dollard *et al.*, 1944) which depict behaviour as being largely governed by the necessity of reducing tensions created by the organism's internal needs. In early medico-psychological models of criminal behaviour (Clarke and Cornish, 1983) the offender was assumed to have a predisposition to offend: deviant motivation acquired as a result of his or her biological inheritance, early learning experiences, or the social environment to which he or she had been exposed. It was such 'internal' criminal propensities, rather than external incentives which were the crucial factors propelling the individual to offend. Should one opportunity for expressing the propensity be blocked, it followed from this essentially hydraulic model of criminal behaviour that the offender would seek either to overcome the obstacle through increased effort or look for alternative ways of achieving his goals by displacing his needs on to other objects.

Two somewhat similar conceptions of criminal behaviour can be derived from such drive models, each predicting displacement-like effects under certain circumstances. In one case, offences might be seen as the varied pathological signs of unchanging but hidden intra-psychic conflicts, with symptom substitution (the commission of functionally-equivalent crimes) as the inevitable result of focussing intervention on these behaviours rather that on the underlying problem (Freud, 1940). Alternatively (cf. Dollard *et al.*, 1944), criminal behaviour could be viewed (in a very general sense) as an aggressive response to frustrating events in the offender's life. Healy and Bronner (1936) explain delinquency in similar terms: lack of satisfying human relationships leads to frustration of important drives, and fuels the urge to seek substitute satisfactions; the failure of these to provide sufficient socially acceptable rewards then propels the individual into delinquent behaviour. Models like these enabled some distinction between so-called 'pathological' and more mundane offending to be made, although both were perhaps better suited to explaining 'expressive' than 'instrumental' offending; hence, no doubt, the role they implicitly play in sociological 'strain' theories of delinquency (Cohen, 1956; Cloward and Ohlin, 1960).

Such models of criminal behaviour also had seemingly clear implications for policy making. Crime control strategies which concentrated only on blocking off the routes to particular criminal activities could expect little real success, since they would merely influence *the mode of expression* of the offender's internal drives or predispositions without in any way tackling the underlying conflict or frustration which continued to energise and motivate offending. At their worst, assumptions about the inevitability of displacement-like effects could lead to a paralysing "extreme-case pessimism" which assumed equal and high levels of criminal propensity on the part of every offender; and which underestimated the plasticity of human behaviour under situational influences. Characteristically, drive models suggested that meaningful reductions in offending could only be achieved by changing the hearts and minds of the criminals themselves.

From drives to incentives
The apparent failure of rehabilitative programmes to reduce crime, however, led to some disenchantment with accounts of offending which seemed to overstress the contribution of internal factors to criminal behaviour. A number of developments in associated disciplines fuelled this dissatisfaction. In academic psychology, Mischel (1968) had attacked the very concept of personality as a useful hypothetical construct, and had drawn attention to the importance of the current

situation in influencing behaviour; while Skinner's radical behaviourism offered a reinforcement-based (i.e. incentive) explanation of human behaviour which both emphasised the importance of current situational variables, and found little use for mental concepts like drives, motives or predispositions. In sociology, too, a large-scale questioning of special motivational accounts of delinquency was taking place (cf. Box, 1981), supported as much from ethnographic accounts of offending as from the insights of control theory (Hirschi, 1969). More pragmatically, policy makers in the area of crime control were stressing the need to produce shorter term policy-relevant research which could be readily translated into practical initiatives. One outcome of these developments was to be the growth of interest in situational crime prevention (cf. Clarke and Cornish, 1983).

Early formulations of situational models, behaviouristic in origin, tended to ignore the offender's perceptions and cognitions. But they have recently been augmented by the introduction of a rational choice perspective. The resulting models still stress the roles of current situational variables, such as opportunities, rewards and costs. But they also take into account the offender's perceptions of these variables and emphasise the essentially rational (if limited) decision-making procedures by means of which their significance to the choice whether or not to offend is evaluated (Clarke and Cornish, 1985).

A new role for the displacement concept

Given the continuing hold over the popular imagination of medico-psychological models of criminal behaviour, it is not surprising that the sorts of displacement effects integral to drive theories of offending should have been vigorously antici-pated by many commentators in relation to these newer situational approaches to crime control. It seems clear that Reppetto (1976) himself initially saw limited potential in "mechanical" crime prevention, believing programmes aimed at changing criminal propensities to be clearly preferable could they but be made to work. Indeed, the explicit use of the term displacement could have all but pre-empted debate about the new measures by once more setting up the image of an offender driven by implacable internal needs to stand against the incentive theorists' "situational" man. Hence, when burglary prevention is being consi-dered, the common belief that target hardening is pointless since, "if he really wants to get in, then he will"; or the unfounded claims about the pervasivness of "soiling" or of irrational acts of vandalism during the course of this offence (cf. Hough and Mayhew, 1983, for empirical data about the prevalence of such behaviours).

Rational choice approaches do, of course, recognise the existence under certain circumstances of displacement-like phenomena. But they seek to explain their presence or absence not in terms of a thwarted predisposition to offend, but in terms of the offender's calculated assessment of the costs and benefits involved. Thus, in the cases previously mentioned, where reduction of subway robberies resulted in an increase of street robberies (Chaiken, *et al.*, 1974), or where target-hardening of one estate displaced a proportion of burglaries to a neighbouring one

4

(Allatt, 1984), it is assumed that the offenders concerned judged the benefits of crime sufficient to make any additional costs worthwhile. On this analysis, whether or not displacement effects occur will depend on the outcome of the criminal's decision-making process (or of the policy maker's success at second-guessing this). In particular, for each case of a situational measure introduced, the question should be asked whether the benefits of crime are enough to compensate for the greater economic and social costs of its commission. In some cases, the answer will clearly be no as shown by a further example: few of the motorists prevented from using illegal tokens in a particular New York district by the introduction of re-designed parking meters were likely to have parked their car in some more distant location simply to save a few pence (cf. Decker, 1972). And costs should not simply be equated with risk or effort. Thus the reason why housewives prevented from shoplifting in their local supermarket by new security measures are unlikely to turn instead to mugging schoolchildren or senior citizens is not just that it may be more inconvenient or risky; in all likelihood it would also be seen by them as a more morally reprehensible act.

In order to understand the empirical manifestations of displacement, then (or indeed to predict or prevent its occurrence), what seems to be needed is a theory of crime which gives a central role to the rational and evaluative components of offender behaviour. In other words the parameters of criminal decisions need to be understood: why it is that particular offenders might contemplate some forms of crime but not others; why certain offences might be preferred at a particular stage in a criminal career; why otherwise law-abiding people sometimes choose to offend; and why a particular target might be selected rather that another one?

Economic theories and some criticisms of the rational perspective

Questions like those above cannot be addressed by most theories of crime. Not only do they neglect the specific costs and benefits and the situational contexts of different forms of crime but, because of their deterministic assumptions, they also generally ignore the offender's conscious thought processes. In at least this latter regard, however, a notable exception is provided by a recently-developed set of theories: the economic theories of crime which deal directly in offenders' decisions. As one of the early exponents has put it: "...a useful theory of criminal behaviour can dispense with special theories of anomie, psychological inadequacies or inheritance of special traits and simply extend the economist's usual analysis of choice" (Becker, 1968). In essence, criminal choices are seen to result when the benefits of crime are judged to exceed the costs in terms of risks and effort.

Unfortunately, economic theories treat crime at too general a level to be of much practical assistance in dealing with issues such as displacement. But they do provide a useful basis on which to construct a more developed theory of criminal choice making use of the results of the large number of crime-specific studies recently carried out by sociologists and criminologists as well as of current research into the psychology of decision making. The general outlines of such a theory are

5

presented below, but first it is necessary to consider a further criticism of economic theories: that they assume too much rationality on the part of the offender.

This criticism has a variety of sources. It may stem, first, from a view of crime as impulsive spur-of-the-moment behaviour prompted by an unexpected opportunity. No doubt some crimes do occur in this way just as there are crimes that require very detailed planning and preparation. Most crimes, however, tend to fall between these extremes, being the result of opportunities which have been sought by an offender who has already made up his mind to commit the offence. (These points have been argued in detail in respect of residential burglaries by Maguire, 1980, and Bennett & Wright, 1984.) And even in the case of more truly opportunistic crimes, the offender still must *decide* to take advantage of the situation.

Second, it might be objected that crimes committed in the heat of anger or passion scarcely seem to fit the rational mould and are more suitably dealt with by drive theories. But many such crimes are, in fact, the end result of what may have been a protracted argument between aggressor and victim during which there may have been numerous opportunities which were not taken to reduce tension or withdraw. Examples of this are to be found in recent research into wife-battering by Dobash & Dobash (1984), and an economic model of violence in the family has recently been developed by Witte, Tauchen and Long (1984). Moreover, interviews undertaken by Athens (1980) with offenders convicted of rape or homicide show clearly that these crimes were usually the result of intentions formed hours, or even days beforehand; they were not the spontaneous eruptions of violence so frequently imagined. Indeed, the picture that emerges from this and other work into the situational contexts of violence is that, however ill-judged, violence is usually a course *chosen* by the offender as a way of solving an interpersonal problem.

Third, it might be pointed out that even ignoring crimes where the offender is clearly suffering from a mental illness, there are some other pathological crimes of sex or violence which by definition are irrational. These unusual offences could never, of course, be representative of crime in general. But in any case their irrationality rests primarily in their motivation and not necessarily in other aspects of the behaviour. Thus, while recognising that there might be room for special motivations (and, hence, drive-theory concepts) as components in any complete explanation of these types of offending, there is still considerable utility in studying the offender's decision-making process. For instance, the offender might exercise considerable care in selecting a suitable victim and show much skill in executing the offence or in covering his tracks. In addition, some offences usually regarded as pathological (e.g. casual homosexual encounters in public lavatories) can often be behaviour encapsulated in an otherwise normal existence (cf. Humphries, 1970). Such acts represent what the offender will judge to be the reasonable risks of gratifying strong and specific needs.

Fourth, it might be said that there are some offences which without being defined as pathological, seem utterly senseless. Such a judgement, however, usually reveals a lack of understanding of offender motivation. Economic theorists, for example, have tended to set too much store on the material, instrumental benefits of crime and too little on its expressive rewards: sexual release, excitement and stimulation, and even friendship or respect. Thus the wanton vandalism committed by the Liverpool youths studied by Gladstone (1978), in reality served the need to demonstrate their toughness or to gain acceptance from their peers. In some cases, the offence also seemed to satisfy a craving for action and excitement. Similar observations have been made in studies of soccer hooliganism (Marsh *et al.*, 1978), which, incidentally, has also been shown not always to be the uncontrollable violence so frequently described by the media; many of the clashes between rival groups of fans are calculated for their maximum effect upon onlookers but usually stop short of deliberately inflicting serious injury. In general, it seems that much apparently senseless crime is in fact calculated to serve the offenders' more-or-less legitimate but unmet needs or wishes.

Finally, it might be objected that it is difficult to regard crime as the outcome of rational decision when the consequences for the offender are so frequently disastrous: arrest, ignominy and punishment, perhaps involving loss of liberty. These are, of course, not the results of crime in the majority of cases: most crimes remain undetected and, even when offenders are caught, the consequences are not always serious. For example, studies in New York City have shown that the typical 'career criminal' has some twelve arrests and eight convictions but in more than half the instances has not received a prison sentence (cf. Reppetto, 1984). But even if the offender is caught and punished, this is not necessarily evidence of his irrationality. He may have been unlucky or he may simply have made the wrong decision and, indeed, he may have done the best he could with the information available. Moreover, as shown in recent psychological research (e.g. Nisbett and Ross, 1980), decision making in the real world is only rarely the deliberate weighing of finely balanced alternatives or the careful analysis of costs and benefits that economic theory portrays. Life is too short and the decisions too many. As a result, people pay attention to only some of the facts at their disposal, they employ short cuts or rules of thumb to speed the decision process, they may perform poorly as a result of fatigue or alcohol, and under pressure of time they may make last-minute changes of plan. No doubt this applies as much to criminal as to other decisions, but none of it implies irrationality. Indeed, it is usually safe to assume that the decisions made represent the offender's best efforts to maximize the benefits for himself.

It might be argued that drive theories could be modified to take into account some of the criticisms implied by the above discussion. For example, a greater recognition of the mundane nature of much crime might reduce the emphasis upon special motivation. This, together with the abandonment of a general theory of criminal behaviour in favour of adopting a less ambitious crime-specific approach, might enable the concepts of "substitute goals" and "threat of punishment" (both made sketchy use of by Miller *et al.*, 1939), and the role of incentives to be more fully developed. But it seems to the present authors that a more fruitful approach is to start from the other end: to assume the commonplace and rational nature of most offending, introducing ideas of special motivation as additions to the model only where needed in the context of particular crimes, and only where their incorporation into the theory is likely to improve the effectiveness of situational measures.

Basic requirements of a choice theory

Because it promotes recognition of the many important differences between crimes, criminal choice theory offers the prospect of being of greater practical assistance in crime prevention than existing theories. Only when a detailed understanding is acquired of the offender's decision making in relation to a particular form of crime will it be possible confidently to put forward preventive measures that are not subject to displacement. Successful crime control may in fact require that much finer distinctions are made between categories of crime than is usual in most statistical recording systems. Thus it may be necessary to distinguish not merely between commercial and residential burglary, but between sub-types of the two categories. For example, burglary on public housing estates may be a quite different problem, requiring different solutions, from burglary in middle-class or affluent areas. In particular, there may be many differences in age, criminal experience, goods sought, planning undertaken and distance travelled among offenders operating in these different locations (cf. Clarke and Hope, 1984). Simple target hardening may be enough to reduce opportunistic burglaries on housing estates where the offenders may be local children, but it may have only a marginal value in reducing burglaries in other locations.

Examples such as these can easily be multiplied and the difficulty lies not so much in appreciating the need for specificity but in deciding just how specific to be. It would seem the touchstone should be a pragmatic one: whether the benefits of prevention are likely to justify the effort of understanding the problem at any given level of specificity. As a footnote to these points it should be said that the emphasis in the choice approach on specificity does not contradict the well-established fact that many persistent offenders engage in a variety of different crimes. For a start, such crimes are not necessarily interchangeable for the offender: the factors influencing their commission may derive from quite different, although sometimes inter-related, sources. (To argue otherwise is again to assume a drive model of offending which makes displacement seem inevitable.) It follows that to explain a particular individual's pattern of criminal activity it may be necessary to draw upon a variety of specific models and to describe the links between them. But the task of accounting for an individual's pattern of offending is in any case different to that of explicitly trying to control particular forms of crime, and the former approach is not necessarily the best route by which to achieve the latter objective. For this purpose, choice theory suggests that in the first instance models should be developed which focus on decision making in relation to specific forms of crime, incorporating additional information about varied offence patterns only where it can be shown (rather than simply assumed) that this will help to improve the devising of 'displacement-free' methods of preventing specific crimes.

An adequate theory of criminal decisions will need, in addition, to illuminate the separate stages in decision making. It will have to be concerned not just with the actual commission of crime, i.e., the *criminal event,* but also with the various stages of involvement that is, with the reasons for the offender's *initial* involvement in crime, and with those factors which influenced his decisions either to *continue* in that form of offending or to *desist.* With an understanding of these four different decision processes, the chances of devising effective situational prevention measures are likely to be much increased.

In the following pages, illustrative models, or flow diagrams, of the four decision processes are presented, drawing extensively upon a formulation published in an earlier paper (Clarke and Cornish, 1985). Instead of attempting to develop very general models that might be adapted for each specific form of crime, the models have been worked out using the example of one particular crime (residential burglary in a middle class suburb). While it might have made more interesting reading to have selected a less obviously instrumental offence, the choice was made for reasons of convenience: familiarity with the considerable amount of research which has recently been conducted on this topic (cf. Clarke and Hope, 1984).

Initial involvement
Figure 1.1 represents the process of initial involvement in residential burglary in a middle class suburb. There are two important decision points: the first (box 7) is the individual's recognition of his 'readiness' to commit this particular offence in order to satisfy certain of his needs for money, goods or excitement. 'Readiness' involves rather more than 'receptiveness': it implies that the inidividual has actually contemplated this form of crime as a solution to his needs, and has decided that under the right circumstances he would commit the offence in question. In reaching this decision, he will have evaluated other ways of satisfying his needs and this evaluation will naturally be influenced by his previous learning experience – his moral code, his view of the kind of person he is, his personal and vicarious experience of crime, and the degree to which he can plan and exercise foresight. These variables are in turn related to various historical and contemporaneous background factors – psychological, familial and socio-demographic (box 1). It is with the influence of these background factors that traditional criminology has been pre-occupied (see Rutter and Giller, 1983, for a recent and comprehensive review); this has sought to determine the values, attitudes and personality traits which dispose the individual to crime. In a decision making context, however, these background influences are less directly criminogenic; instead they have an orienting function – exposing people to particular problems and particular opportunities and leading them to perceive and evaluate these in particular (criminal) ways. Moreover, the contribution of background factors to the final decision to commit crime would be much moderated by situational and transitory influences; and for certain sorts of crime (e.g. computer fraud) the individual's background might be of much less relevance than his immediate situation.

The second decision (box 8), actually to commit a burglary, is precipitated by

9

Figure 1.1 Initial involvement model

(Example: Burglary in a middle class suburb)

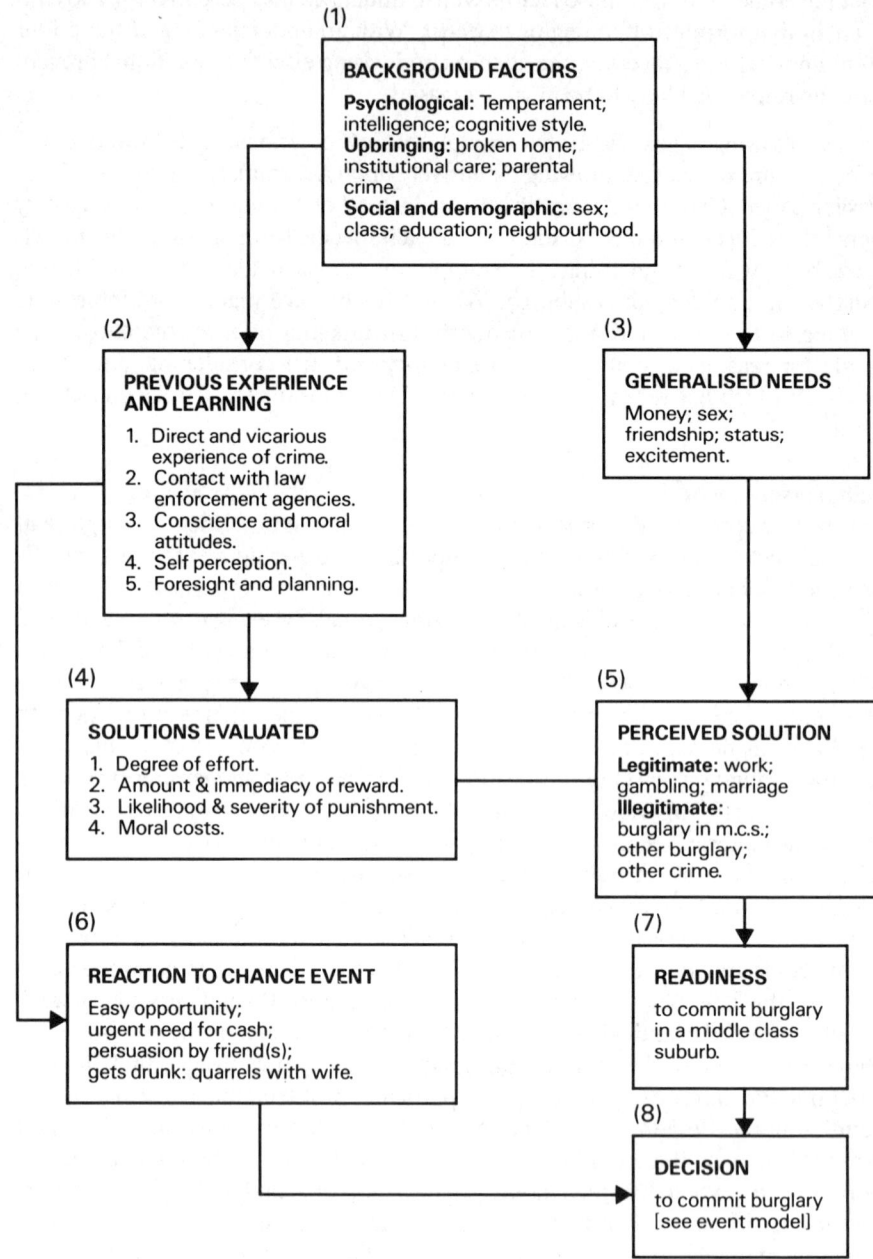

some chance event. The individual may suddenly need money, he may have been drinking with associates who suggest committing a burglary (for many offences, especially those committed by juveniles, immediate pressure from the peer group is important), or he may perceive an easy opportunity for the offence during the course of his routine activities (cf. Maguire, 1982; Bennett and Wright, 1984). In real life, of course, the two decision points may occur almost simultaneously and the chance event may not only precipitate the decision to burgle, but may also play a part in the perception and evaluation of solutions to generalized needs.

The criminal event

Figure 1.2 depicts the further sequence of decision making which leads the burglar to select a particular house: particularly important will be the burglar's estimate of the likely haul, his judgement about whether anyone is likely to be at home, and his assessment of how easy it would be to affect entry and egress without being seen by neighbours or passers-by (Winchester and Jackson, 1982). For some other kinds of crime, the sequence will be much lengthier; and the less specific the offence being modelled, the more numerous the alternative choices. For example, should a more general model of burglary be required, a wider range of areas and housing types would have to be included (cf. Brantingham and Brantingham, 1978). In the

Figure 1.2   Event model

(Example: Burglary in a middle class suburb)

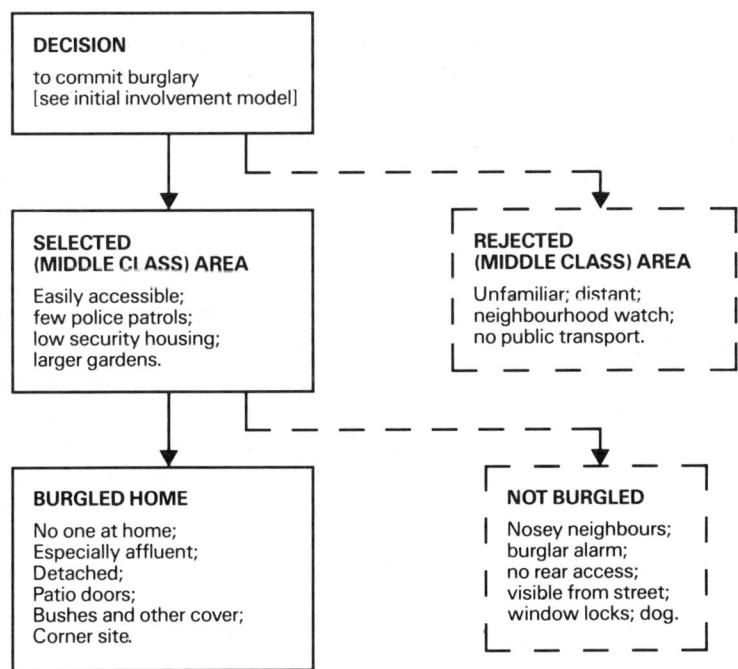

present case, however, there may be little choice of area in which to work, and in time this decision, and perhaps elements of later decisions, may become routine.

This is, of course, an idealized picture of burglars' decision making. Where the formal complexity of the decision task is laid out in detail, as in Walsh's (1978, 1980) work, there may be a temptation to assume that it entails equally complex decision making. But in real life only patchy and inaccurate information will be available and under these uncertain circumstances the offender's perceptions, his previous experience, his fund of criminal lore and the characteristic features of his information-processing become crucial to the decision reached. Moreover, the external situation itself may alter during the timespan of the decision sequence. The result is that the decision process may be telescoped, and planning may be rudimentary. Even this account may over-emphasize the deliberate element since alcohol may cloud judgement (Bennett and Wright, 1984). Only research into these aspects of criminal decision making will provide event models sufficiently detailed and accurate to assist policy making.

Continuance

Interviews with burglars have shown that in many cases they may commit hundreds of offences (see, for example, Maguire 1982); the process of continuing involvement in burglary is represented in Figure 1.3. It is assumed here that, as a result of generally positive reinforcement, the frequency of offending increases until it reaches (or subsequently reduces to) some optimum level (cf. Rengert, in press). But is is possible to conceive of more or less intermittent patterns of involvement for some individuals; and intermittent patterns may be more common for other types of offence (for instance, those for which ready opportunities occur less frequently). It is unlikely that each time the offender sets out to commit an offence he will actively consider the alternatives, though this will sometimes be necessary as a result of a change in his circumstances or in the conditions under which his burglaries have to be committed. (These possibilities are discussed in more detail in regard to the desistance model of Figure 1.4.)

Of greater importance to the continuance model are the gradually changing conditions and personal circumstances that confirm the offender in his readiness to commit burglary. The diagram summarizes three inter-related categories of relevant variables. The first concerns an increase in professionalism: pride in improved skills and knowledge; successive reductions of risk and an improvement in haul through planning and careful selection of targets; and the acquisition of reliable fencing contacts. The second reflects some concomitant changes in lifestyle: a recognition of increased financial dependence on burglary; a choice of legitimate work to facilitate burglary (cf. Rengert, in press); enjoyment of "life in the fast-lane" (cf. Gibbs and Shelly, 1982); the devaluation of ordinary work; and the development of excuses and justifications for criminal behaviour (cf. Matza's, 1964, "techniques of neutralization"). Thirdly, there will be changes in the offender's network of peers and associates and his relationship to the 'straight' world.

Figure 1.3   Continuing involvement model

(Example: Burglary in a middle class suburb)

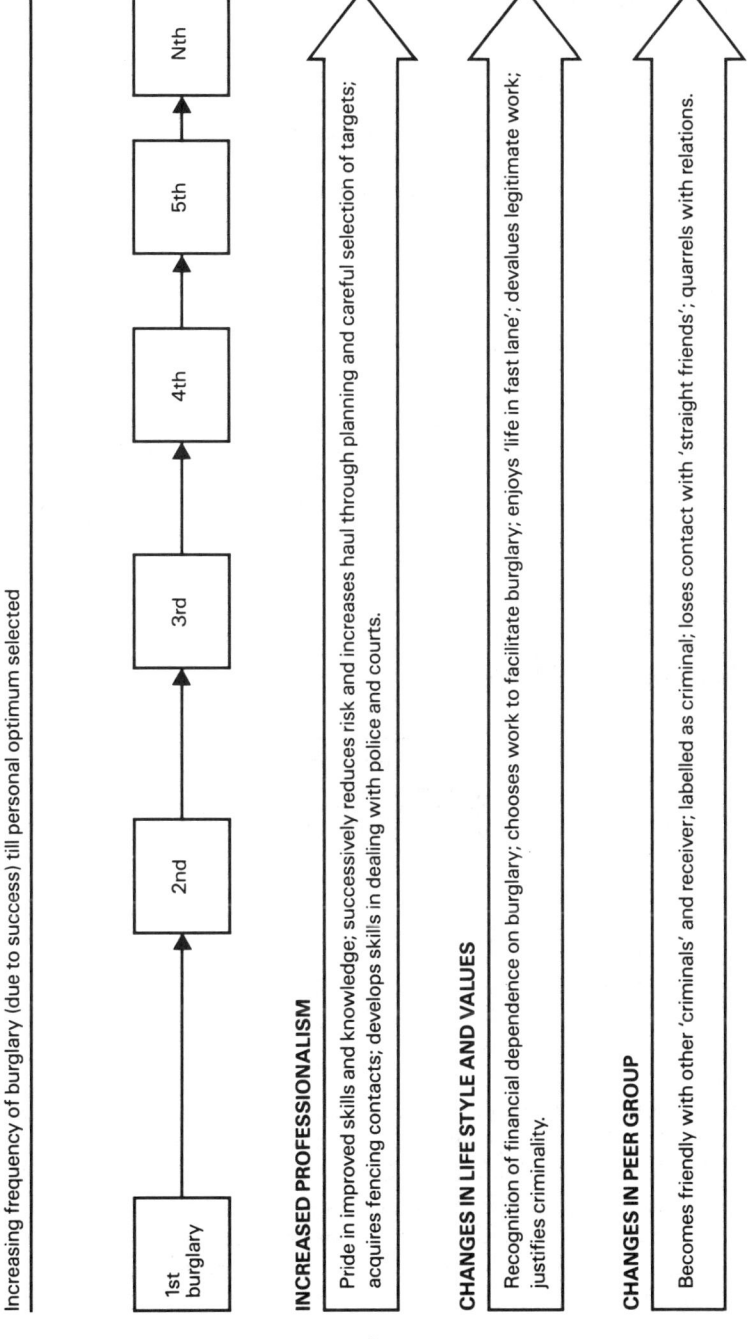

Increasing frequency of burglary (due to success) till personal optimum selected

1st burglary → 2nd → 3rd → 4th → 5th → Nth

INCREASED PROFESSIONALISM

Pride in improved skills and knowledge; successively reduces risk and increases haul through planning and careful selection of targets; acquires fencing contacts; develops skills in dealing with police and courts.

CHANGES IN LIFE STYLE AND VALUES

Recognition of financial dependence on burglary; chooses work to facilitate burglary; enjoys 'life in fast lane'; devalues legitimate work; justifies criminality.

CHANGES IN PEER GROUP

Becomes friendly with other 'criminals' and receiver; labelled as criminal; loses contact with 'straight friends'; quarrels with relations.

These trends may be accelerated by criminal convictions as opportunities to obtain ligitimate work decrease and as ties to family and relations are weakened.

Figure 1.4   Desistance model

(Example: Burglary in a middle class suburb)

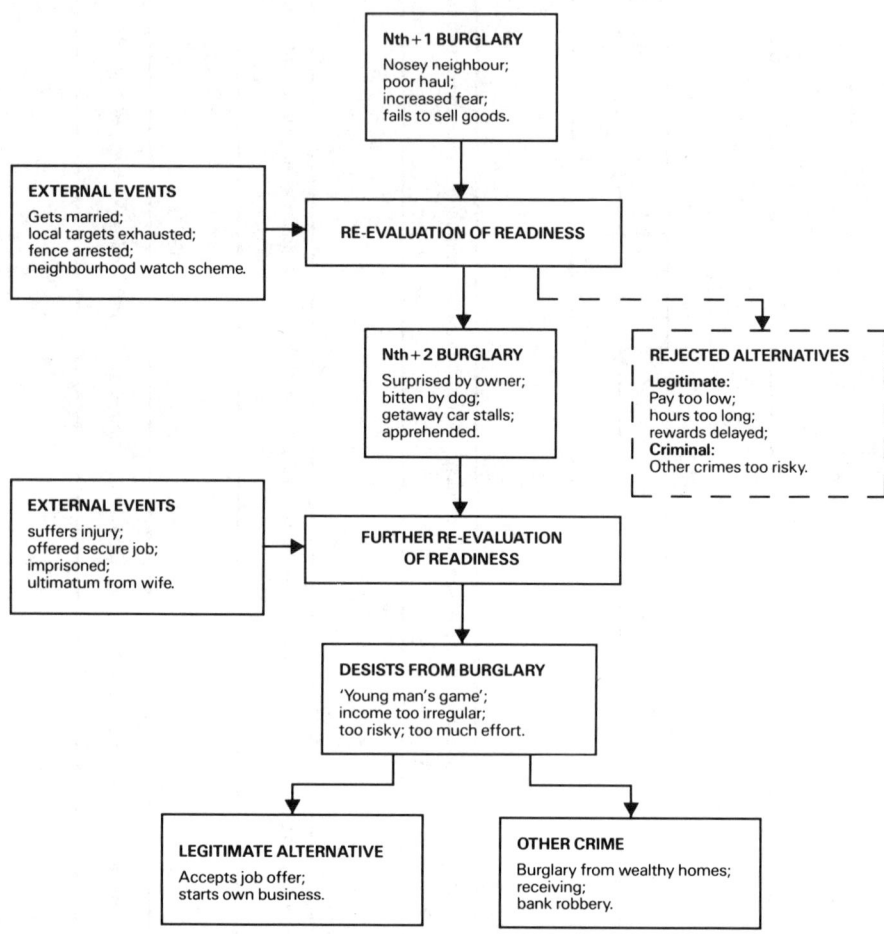

Desistance

There is a paucity of relevant criminological information in respect of the offender's desistance from burglary. While the work of, for example, Greenberg (1977), Maguire (1982), Parker (1974), Trasler (1979), Gordon West (1978) and Donald West (1982) provide some understanding of the process of desistance, empirical data, whether relating to groups or individuals or in respect of particular sorts of crime, are very scanty. Nevertheless, there is sufficient information to provide in Figure 1.4 an illustration of the offender's decision processes as he begins a renewed evaluation of alternatives to burglary. This follows aversive experiences during the course of offending (being disturbed by a returning householder, being pursued by neighbours) and changes in his personal circumstances (age, marital status, financial requirements) and the neighbourhood and community context in which he operates (changes in policing; depletion of potential targets). These result in his abandoning burglary in favour of some alternative solution, either legitimate or criminal. While desistance may imply the cessation of all criminal activity, in other cases it may simply represent displacement to some other target (commercial premises rather than houses) or to another form of crime. Desistance is, in any case, not necessarily permanent and may simply be part of a continuing process of lulls in the offending of persistent criminals (West, 1963) or even, perhaps, of a more casual drifting in and out of particular crimes.

Conclusions

Whatever the imperfections of the models presented and however rudimentary the level of theorizing, the discussion above does permit a number of important conclusions to be drawn. First, it is clear that rational choice theories of crime are capable of being developed so as to (a) include expressive as well as instrumental goals, (b) take proper account of fundamental differences between crime types, and (c) explain the different stages of criminal involvement as well as the criminal event itself. Second, a theory of crime premised upon individual choice can quite easily be reconciled with the empirical facts yielded by what has for the most part been a deterministic criminology. Third, not only can choice theory accommodate the facts of traditional criminology, but it can easily take on board the findings and concepts of deviancy sociology which, after all, has concerned itself largely with the offender's perceptions and point of view. Fourth, and most importantly, criminal choice theory is capable of providing answers to many questions lying outside the scope of conventional criminology concerning such matters as temporal and geographical patterns of crime, the isolated offending of otherwise law-abiding people, and changes of course in criminal careers.

Choice theory thus has considerable value in encompassing and systematizing both current theory and available empirical knowledge. But this is essentially an academic benefit whereas the purpose of the present discussion was to demonstrate choice theory's practical value for crime control. In particular, it was argued above that it should provide a better basis than conventional criminology for predicting and even preventing displacement. This it can do by helping to identify the questions that need to be answered in respect of any single preventive measure: how does the offender think it alters the risks of crime? And of which crimes in particular? How much extra effort will he see it as demanding in respect of a particular offence type? Will he still judge the pay-off to be worthwhile? If not, what other kinds of crime might he entertain? What would be the costs for society of his alternative courses of action? What would be the likely long-term effect on his criminal career? And how else apart from crime could he earn a living or meet his other needs? In short, the four models comprising choice theory should help to provide an understanding of the ways in which preventive measures are perceived and evaluated by those who are the intended targets of crime control policies. Without this understanding the history of crime control will continue to be a catalogue of failure.

To answer the questions above will demand fresh research perhaps along the lines of the crime specific studies recently conducted of residential burglary. In the course of this work on burglary a variety of topics relevant to choice theory have been investigated. These include judgements about suitable targets (Reppetto, 1974; Maguire, 1982; Bennett and Wright, 1984); the lives and daily routines of repeat offenders (Rengert, in press); the rewards of a burglary career (Gibbs and Shelly, 1982); the life histories of career burglars (Maguire, 1982); and preferred frequencies of offending (Rengert, in press; Bennett and Wright, 1984). Research into these and other aspects of criminal choice will demand a mix of research methods including qualitative ethnographic, case study and interviewing techniques as well as some quantitative methods less familiar to criminology such as time budgeting and daily logs, process tracing (Payne, 1980), and frequent reinterviewing of small cohorts. Whatever the value of choice theory, research of this kind will greatly enhance understanding of a number of criminology's traditional concerns: for example, offender motivation, criminal careers and situational influences on crime. This store of new knowledge may indeed prove to be choice theory's most enduring criminological legacy for, like all good theories, it should contain the seeds of its own destruction: whatever its immediate practical value the facts it helps to produce ought in time to provide the building-blocks for some more sophisticated and (temporarily) more satisfying theory of crime.

2 Situational crime control and rational choice: a critique

Gordon Trasler

In the volume *Designing Out Crime* Clarke and Mayhew (1980) brought together an impressive collection of papers concerned with the 'situational' prevention of crime by eleven members of the Home Office Research and Planning Unit. The papers described a variety of methods of protecting people and their possessions, ranging from target hardening, surveillance and police patrolling – methods of crime prevention in the tradition established by Newman (1972), Jeffrey (1971,1977), Sagalyn (1973) and others. Clarke criticised contemporary preoccupation with 'dispositional' theories of crime (that is to say, theories which concentrate on the alleged differences between criminals and others) on the grounds they do not generate practical policies for the reduction of crime.

Clarke and Mayhew's book was essentially atheoretical, concentrating upon methods and techniques in preventing crime. However, Clarke and Cornish (1985) (see also Cornish and Clarke, Chapter 1) have developed what they refer to as a 'rational choice model', essentially a theory of criminal behaviour, which they offer as an appropriate theoretical basis for situational crime prevention, and a more fruitful approach to the explanation of criminal behaviour.

The purpose of this chapter is to explore the extent and the limits of situational crime prevention; to examine Clarke's characterisation of 'dispositional' theories of criminality as sterile with respect to practical methods of controlling crime; and lastly to consider the 'rational choice model' proposed by Clarke and Cornish.

Limitations to designing out crime

There are some kinds of crime that can be controlled by making changes in the environment and its furniture, for example, criminal damage or vandalism. The target-hardening measures such as strengthening coin boxes in public telephone booths, modifying pre-payment meters in domestic electricity and town gas supplies, replacing vulnerable glass street-lamp lenses with damage-resistant plastic materials, and lining pedestrian underpasses with readily cleanable ceramic tiles, are fairly effective in coping with the obvious aspects of criminal behaviour but they can be costly and of limited impact in the longer term.

To pursue this point, there seems to be little agreement concerning public attitudes to damage and defacement of property. While the damage itself is of little moment, broken widows and walls defaced by aerosol-painted slogans are interpreted by many people as indications of lawlessness, incivility, and urban

17

decay and so assume greater importance than one might expect. As a result very large sums of money have been spent on endeavours to contain vandalism (the campaign to erase graffiti on the subway system of New York City is a case in point) but although it is probably justifiable to regard the proliferation of graffiti as an index of incivility, it would be quite wrong to assume that erasure of graffiti would of itself have a long term impact on reversing the process of urban decay. Thus while situational interventions to restrain vandalism may be effective, they are expensive and of limited value in attempts to mitigate the distress associated with crime in inner-city areas.

Displacement

Whether measures for the environmental control of crime, introduced as an experiment are to be counted as a success depends, firstly, on whether they have succeeded in reducing the incidence of the target crime in the area in which the trial takes place, and secondly, on whether displacement has occurred. Many studies of environmental crime prevention have ignored, or have taken too simple a view of, the phenomenon of displacement. An increase in the incidence of burglaries or street crimes in areas adjacent to those in which the experiment was carried out is commonly used as an index of displacement: in most planned interventions displacement effects of this kind have been difficult to identify. (There is some evidence that a campaign to reduce the incidence of 'mugging' – robbery from the person by the use or threat of violence – may have led to displacement from platform crime to robbery in trains, which had previously been regarded as a safe means of urban transport.)

However, as Hakim and Rengert (1981) point out, there are at least five types of displacement, some of which are a great deal more difficult to measure than simple geographical spillover. These include, in addition to 'spatial displacement' (the offender moving to another neighbourhood where environmental control measures have not been adopted), 'temporal displacement' (changing the time of day, the day, or the season to one in which criminal activity is safer), 'tactical displacement', where the criminal varies his techniques *(modus operandi)* to reduce the risk of being caught by the new measures; 'target displacement', in which the offender looks for easier targets, when, for example, effective burglar alarms or neighbourhood watch schemes have been introduced, and 'type of crime displacement', when criminals abandon what has become a high-risk crime, because of environmental control programmes, and turn instead to crimes which seem to be less risky. Each of these four kinds of 'crime spillover' is very hard to measure, and the lack of systematic data on the careers of individual criminals in Britain make 'type of crime displacement' very difficult to demonstrate. The Rand studies (Petersilia, Greenwood and Lavin, 1978; Peterson, Braiker and Polich, 1980) and the Racine research (Shannon, 1978; Olson, 1972) do provide some interesting data, but it has to be said that we are a long way from measuring 'crime switch', and even further from measuring, with any precision, the extent to which offenders' choices of targets, methods and kinds of crime are sensitive to changes in the risk of being apprehended and the severity of the punishment that would follow conviction.

18

An example of substantial target hardening (the most popular situational measure) is the extensive use of security firms (such as Securicor) to transport large quantities of cash and other valuables. Such agencies use specially strengthened vehicles and guards with protective headgear and clothing, and they have elaborate procedures to minimise the risk of robbery. There does not appear to be any evidence that the use of such private security carriers has resulted in a fall in the incidence of robberies of this kind; on the other hand, it seems to have raised the level of violence or threat involved in such robberies. In that sense there has been an escalation rather than prevention. There are other examples of adaptation to the new circumstances represented by target hardening: the payment of wages by cheque generally requires a computer-based system, thus extending opportunites for computer frauds.

There have been many attempts to restrain shoplifters and dishonest employees, including surveillance systems and local networks of store detectives who collaborate in apprehending offenders. Some stores (mainly in the fashion and clothing trade) make use of magnetic devices which set off an alarm if a customer tries to take the garment through the exit doors without paying: the checkout assistant normally deactivates or removes the device at the point of payment. Again, there is no evidence that these precautions have actually reduced the incidence of shoplifting – perhaps because the selling tactics of stores require conditions, such as the unsupervised display of goods, which are not compatible with the most powerful methods for the control of theft. It is estimated that the annual stock loss from shoplifting and employee theft in Britain is in excess (possibly greatly in excess) of one billion pounds *per annum*. Better monitoring of store stocks, which would presumably reduce pilfering by customers and sales staff, would clearly reduce such losses. But whether the protection gained would outweigh restrictions imposed on ordinary commercial activity is at least a moot point.

Similar consideration may be given to what has come to be called 'autocrime' (theft of motor vehicles or of the contents of motor vehicles, notably radio and audio-tape equipment). It has been established that the legal requirement to fit steering-column locks on new cars substantially reduced the incidence of theft of these vehicles, but in the United Kingdom at least there was also a displacement effect, so that the risk of interference with vehicles manufactured before the introduction of steering column locks was considerably increased.

Econometric models and rational crime

While it is true that psychologists concentrating on the temperamental characteristics of offenders have made modest (but not negligible) contributions to practical measures to deal with crime (Clarke, 1983) there is good reason to be wary of claims for the practical utility and theoretical potential of representations of crime as rational, utilitarian decision making. The models developed by econometricians represent one kind of rational choice model, based upon the notion of maximisation of gain and the minimisation of risk, and seem limited in explanatory value. In particular such models do not offer a convincing characterisation of the kinds of crimes about which many people are most concerned. For example, it does not fit crimes of passion or expressive crimes such as most homicides or rapes. Ehrlich's (1975) attempts to measure the general deterrent effects of executions of people convicted of murder, for example, seem very unconvincing to some criminologists, given the information we currently have about the sequence of events which typically leads to a homicide. (Beyleveld, 1982; Sellin, 1980; see also Ehrlich's reply to Beyleveld's criticisms in the same volume.) Rational consideration of the probable consequences of a homicide does not seem to be a frequent element in crimes of murder. The same may be true of other expressive crimes. Thus major (and well publicised) increases in sentences for rape do not appear to have had any measurable influence on the frequency and the degree of brutality of crimes of this kind in Philadelphia (Schwartz, 1968; see also West, Roy and Nicholls, 1978, and West 1983).

The concept of rational choice

As Cook (1980) points out, the notion of rational choice has its origins in fairly recent economic theory, although Bentham saw the appropriateness of utilitarian analysis in explaining the circumstances in which a given individual will commit a crime: "The profit of the crime is the force which urges a man to delinquency: the pain of the punishment is the force employed to restrain him from it. If the first of these forces is the greater the crime will be committed; if the second, the crime will not be committed". (Cook, 1980). But the doctrine of rational choice as applied to criminal conduct does not require full rationality, that is to say, the capacity to examine every opportunity to commit a crime and to weigh probable gain against the probable risk of incurring a penalty. The concept of limited rationality recognises the limited capacity of many (or most) individuals to acquire and process information, and makes use of 'standing decisions' i.e. habitual responses or dispositions which govern the individual's response to opportunities for crime, in ordinary circumstances. Cook remarks that "most of us have long ago adopted standing decisions to refrain from robbery and assault, no matter what the circumstances" (Cook 1980). There seems to be similarities between the notion of 'standing decisions' and the psychologist's concept of internalised inhibitions (see Trasler, 1978).

The distinction that Cook makes between rationality in the full utilitarian (Benthamite) sense, and standing decisions seems to be a useful one. What have been identified as 'spillover' effects seem to relate to those crimes which involve calcualtions (or guesses) about potential gains and the risks and consequences of apprehension: such considerations clearly apply to instrumental crimes, and particularly those committed by habitual offenders; they give no guidance to those who seek to reduce the level of violent crime, and especially those who commit, and attempt murder, rape and other so-called expressive crimes. To put the matter bluntly, they may be of some help in designing defences against property crimes, but offer little protection against those violent offences that cause most apprehension, distress, and fear of further victimisation.

The definition of decision making adopted by Clarke and Cornish is closely similar to that used by the deterrence theorists: "...the conscious thought processes that give purpose to and justify conduct, and the underlying cognitive mechanisms by which information about the world is selected, attended to, and processed" (Clarke and Cornish, 1985). Whether offenders actually do this is an empirical question which would be difficult to resolve.

Clarke and Cornish's approach makes use of the term rational choice or rational decision making at several levels. The decision to abandon criminal activity, which may be based upon a realistic assessment of the probable consequences of continuing in crime (such as losing one's home or one's job) is perhaps an example of careful, purposive weighing of opportunities and risks. However, studies of criminal careers suggest that for many offenders initial involvement in thefts or burglaries can seldom be described as a decision to take up such a career; people drift into criminal activities, influenced by the encouragement of their peers, or because they see opportunities for enriching themselves at small risk of getting caught; commitment to crime is something that emerges gradually. Clarke and Cornish also use the term rational choice to describe burglars' choices of targets, shoplifters' preferences for large self-service stores, and vandals' concentration upon public property, such as telephone kiosks. Such decisions may be based on previous experience (successful or unsuccessful) the advice of others, or simply a desire to stick with methods that are well-practiced and familiar. Whether it is helpful to regard these very difficult kinds of decisions, which "...need separately to describe both the processes of involvement in crime and the decisions surrounding the commission of the offence itself" as examples of the rational decision process is a matter for debate.

Studies of criminal careers

Clarke has criticised what he sees as the preoccupation of contemporary criminology with research aimed at identifying the causes of crime because "...theories (which seek) to explain why some individuals or groups are born with, or come to acquire, a 'disposition' to offend" seem, for practical policies of crime control, very unhelpful: that is to say, they (for the most part) identify the antecedent events which seem to be connected to later criminality (for example, deprivation or parental affection, or growing up in an underprivileged family) which cannot subsequently be put right. There is no way of reversing such events when the disposition to get into trouble eventually manifests itself in adolescence. He also reminds us that attempts to control crime by subjecting offenders to 'treatment', and by individual and general deterrence, have been unsuccessful. There are certainly grounds for devoting more attention and more resources to the strategies of situational crime prevention. But it would be most unfortunate if, persuaded by pessimism about treatment, studies of the individual offender were abandoned. There seem to be major categories of crime, including some of those that are a source of great public concern, which are not amenable to situational crime prevention. These include most of the so-called expressive crimes, and some of the

21

instrumental crimes, such as robbery.

Studies of individual offenders (for example, those by Maguire (1982), Bennett (1984) and Walsh (1980)), have yielded useful information about the judgements which determine whether someone will attempt a burglary, which clearly has relevance to crime control policies. We need comparable studies of street robbery, and of vandalism, which will tell us about the way in which the individual interprets various cues, such as (in the case of robbery) things that indicate that the proposed victim is a stranger in town, unlikely to put up strong resistance, or otherwise a 'safe' target; and (in the case of vandalism) the way in which the commission of a single visible act of damage invites others to join in.

It is true that some crime is committed casually, on the spur of the moment, or under unusual conditions of stress or the encouragement of others, by people who are unlikely to repeat the experience if, as a result, they are arrested and taken to court. But it is also clear that a large proportion of crimes such as burglary, robbery and other forms of theft are committed by a comparatively small group of persistent offenders who typically show a high rate of offending, a low risk of apprehension, and relatively little specialisation. We need to know much more about these people, their decision-making processes, what makes them persist, and (most important of all) why they eventually abandon their criminal careers.

It may be that we are too pessimistic about the practicality of identifying such people, perhaps not at the outset of their careers, but certainly before mid-career. The transitional probabilities found in the Racine study (Olson, 1972; Shannon, 1978; see also Petersilia, 1980) and the Rand research (Greenwood, 1984; Greenwood, Petersilia and Zimring 1980; Petersilia, Greenwood and Lavin 1978; Petersilia and Greenwood 1978; Peterson, Braiker and Polich 1980) seem to show that there comes a point quite early in the series of convictions at which the probability of further repeated offending becomes so high that special intervention is required. Clarke is right in asserting that conventional forms of 'treatment' are futile and likely to remain so. Incapacitation by prolonged incarceration is a very unattractive course, and certainly expensive, but it has its advocates. A third possibility (and this is one reason for emphasising the need to study why such people eventually give up crime) might take the form of individualised deterrence, that is, the threat of a sanction which the particular individual would fear. At present the courts act by guesswork and by rules of thumb. They could be more effective if we knew more about this group of highly active career criminals.

We need, in Kelly's terms, to establish the range and focus of convenience of the Clarke and Cornish theory, and the relationship between rational choice and a determinist model of criminal behaviour. Clarke and Cornish have some important things to say about the scope, power and range of competing, or possibly co-existing and complementary models of crime. But we need to explore further the limits of the theory they propose for, as we have already indicated, while rational choice models may reasonably fit property crimes, such as burglary, they do not help us with expressive crimes, such as homicide or rape. Nor is it entirely clear

22

whether the rational choice model is an empirical statement (that is to say, criminal actions are predictable, given certain information about the circumstances which obtain on a particular occasion), or a hypothetical statement (a proposed theory implies that criminal actions will occur in certain circumstances and not in others: the degree of success that attends crime prevention operations based upon this theory will furnish a test of the basic premises of the theory). We need to ask, what is the practical value of the rational choice model? What does it enable us to do?

To what extent do we have to make a choice between situational and dispositional crime prevention? In the case of expressive crimes of violence, there are few practical preventive precautions we can take. By contrast, there is growing evidence that selective incapitation might considerably curtail the level of instrumental crimes, albeit at considerable cost, in money terms, and particularly in the human cost of 'false positives'.

These considerations seem to point to several rather general conclusions:
(i)   it is a mistake to view situational crime prevention schemes as alternatives to dispositional, incapacitative methods; indeed, the difficulty of achieving situational control of some types of crime emphasises the value of incapacitative strategies;
(ii) the rational choice model is in essence the familiar utilitarian analysis of human conduct, which emphasises the extent to which men and women seek to maximise the yield of their actions, in terms of financial gain, and to minimise the risks of loss and judicial penalty;
(iii) if criminal behaviour were wholly rational in the economists' sense, it would be (at least in principle) wholly preventable by the imposition of penalties sufficiently severe to outweigh expected gains divided by judged risks of conviction and sentence. The inefficiency of the criminal justice system in restraining crime may partly reflect the low level of reporting, detection and conviction in the major categories of property crime, but probably also fails to take account of the small group of high-frequency, systematic property offenders who are responsible for a very large proportion of all instrumental crime (i.e. crimes that are profitable in terms of the financial risk of detection and yield) whose judgements of the risks of apprehension are approximately accurate. It is not necessary, in practice, to assess whether their calculations of risk and potential gain are accurate: it is only neccesary to identify individuals whose estimates of the probable balance of gains (profits) and losses (convictions and periods of incapacitation) are comparatively optimistic, in relation to the known statistics of clear-up rates and the going rate of incapacitative penalties. If it were possible to identify the individual offender who got this calculation wrong (this is to say, who underestimated the likelihood and consequences of detection) the essential problem of differential incapacitation would be solved. But we do not as yet have the data upon which such a policy could be based.

Policies of crime reduction really demand two strategies: deterring occasional or low-rate offenders from committing crimes (especially, but not exclusively, instrumental crimes) and identifying and incapacitating high-rate, persistent offenders. Situational crime control offers effective measures for the first group, but is likely to have little impact on the second group.

3 A model for action

Barry Poyner

For many years road accidents have been the subject of research which has illustrated, among other things, the value of studying the association between the
behaviour of the individual (for example the car driver) and the situation within
which the accident takes place. The approach used in this work is relevant to the
study of crime and its prevention.

After the first section of motorway was opened in Britain in 1959, there were a
number of accidents at the motorway terminals (Department of Scientific and
Industrial Research, 1962). At that time all terminals were designed in the form
of roundabout junctions. When the accidents were plotted at these junctions, as in
figure 3.1, it was clear that there was a particular problem for drivers of vehicles
leaving the motorway.

If we look at this problem in a similar way to which many people look at crime, we
could blame these accidents on 'bad' drivers. Indeed, we might be right. The accidents could be caused by less competent drivers or even by drivers who deliberately drive dangerously, but it will be almost impossible to find out if this is true.
All we know for certain is that the vehicles had failed to stay on the road or collided
with other vehilces at the roundabout.

We might also go on to seek explanations for these accidents. Perhaps the relatively high speeds on the motorway make it difficult for some drivers to decide the
best speed to approach the roundabout, or maybe their perception of speed
becomes distorted after prolonged driving at the same high speed. Some drivers
may be half asleep due to the effects of continuous driving at the same speed in a
poorly ventilated car. We may gain some clues about these explanations from
interviewing drivers, but it is unlikely that we can ever be certain about such explanations. Even if we are certain about these explanations, they do little to help us
decide what we have to do to prevent the accidents.

Those responsible for accident research did not seek to blame the accidents on
'bad' drivers nor did they look for possible explanations in terms of factors such as
high speed or weariness. What they did was to recognise that the particular conditions created by this design of a motorway terminal *increased the risk* of accidents.
By changing the conditions at the end of the motorway they believed that the risk
might be reduced (even for the 'bad' drivers). What was proposed was that subsequent motorway terminals should be designed without roundabouts. The end of
a motorway was to be gradually merged with an existing trunk road and any junc-

Figure 3.1   Approximate position of accidents at four principal terminals of the London-Birmingham Motorway (1959-1961)

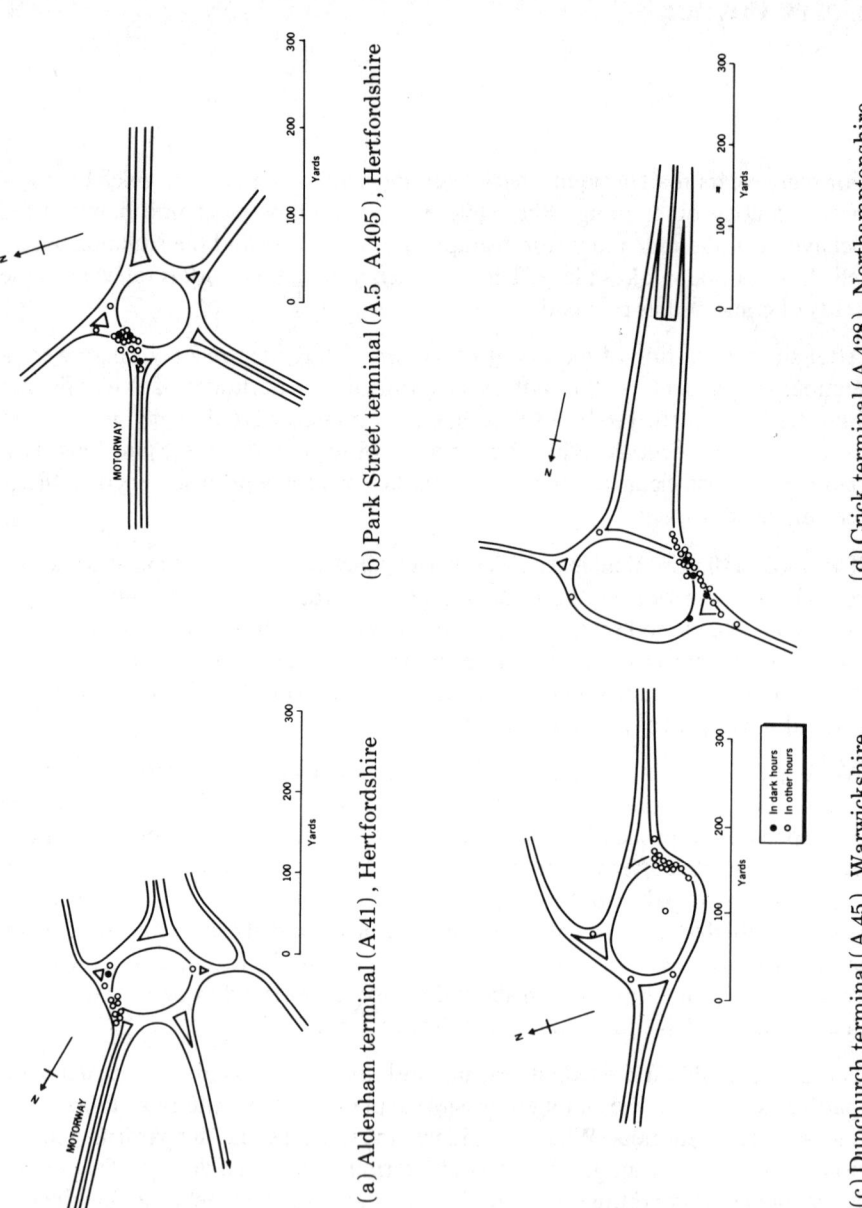

(a) Aldenham terminal (A.41), Hertfordshire

(b) Park Street terminal (A.5 A.405), Hertfordshire

(c) Dunchurch terminal (A.45), Warwickshire

(d) Crick terminal (A.428), Northamptonshire

tions at this point were to be designed as other motorway junctions with slip roads and grade separation. The result of this new form of motorway terminal was that few accidents occurred. Since then most new motorway terminals have been designed in this way.

This example from road safety research provides us with a valuable paradigm for crime prevention. Whereas efforts directed at trying to change people's behaviour or to understand the underlying reasons for crime have been found relatively ineffective, it may be that efforts directed at changing the conditions under which crimes occur will be much more fruitful. The purpose of this paper is to describe a research model for crime prevention which adopts this approach. The model is currently being used in research on crime. It has been developed from similar models used in accident research (Poyner, 1980a).

Knowledge of incidents
The first step in developing the model is to set down as much as we can about each incident of crime. The most obvious source of information on crime are police files. The information available will vary greatly, depending on the nature of the incident and the extent to which it has been witnessed. There may be little that can be recorded about a shop window found broken in a shopping centre if no one had either heard or seen anything and if there was no sign of any goods having been stolen. By contrast, a running fight between two groups of youths in a town centre may have been witnessed by many people including the police and, if at least some of the youths were later interviewed by the police, a quite detailed account of what happened can be pieced together.

In order to set down information about incidents in an orderly way, experience suggests that material can be conveniently organised under the following headings:

What happened – we may only know that some damage has been done or that something has been stolen, but we may have a detailed account of a series of events which led up to the crime as well as subsequent events.

Where it happened – the exact location is not always known; sometimes a sequence of events takes place in several locations.

When the events occurred – we may only know the period of time in which the events occurred or we may know precisely when each event occurred.

Who was involved – there will always be at least one offender and there may be several; there may be one or more victims even if they are not involved directly with the offender; there may be witnesses and other third parties.

Physical environment – this will include the physical form of the environment and its relationship to its surrounding; it will also include the conditions found at the time (e.g. weather, time, lighting).

Social environment – who else is about at the time of the incident and what they were doing; crowds, police, people who might intervene or report criminal activity.

Police records are often inadequate to provide all this information, but it is worth studying statements made to the police by offenders, victims and other witnesses, if they are available. They often mention details which would not be routinely recorded, such as the weather if that had some influence on the crime or that the victim may have spent the earlier part of the evening drinking in a number of pubs.

Several fruitful avenues for further data collection are open to researchers. Easiest of all is to revisit the scenes of the incidents, and it is often revealing to do so at the same time and day of the week as the incident occurred. It is increasingly popular among researchers to interview offenders and victims. All such sources are helpful, particularly if they concentrate on more objective aspects of incidents rather than exploring the reasons or feelings behind the events. The difficulty with using data from offenders and victims is that relatively few offenders are known to the police and many crimes do not involve victims directly (e.g. most burglaries).

The process model

Although there are considerable differences in the amount of information that can be assembled for different crimes, it is helpful to represent this information systematically. To do this a diagrammatic representation of crimes has been evolved as shown in figure 3.2.

Figure 3.2   Process model of crimes

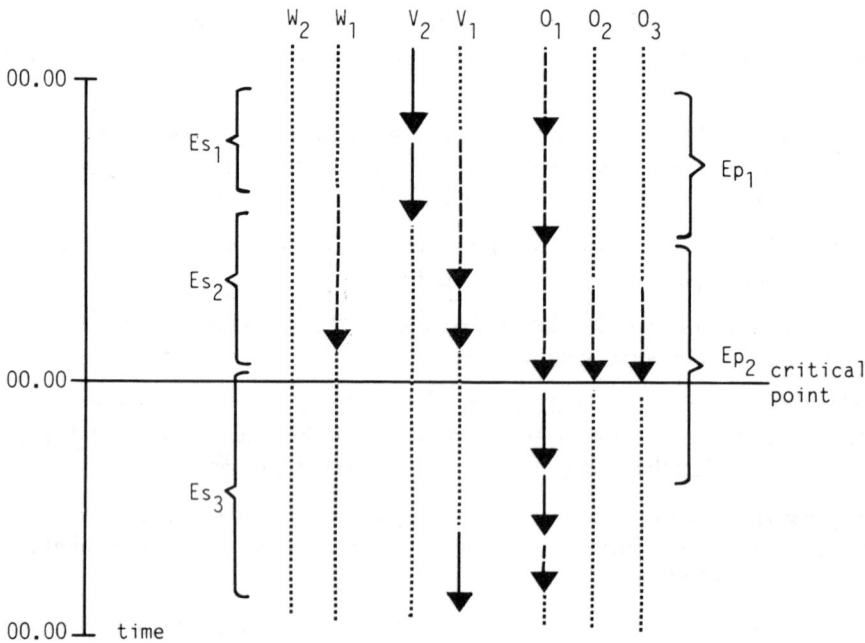

Figure 3.3   A car theft

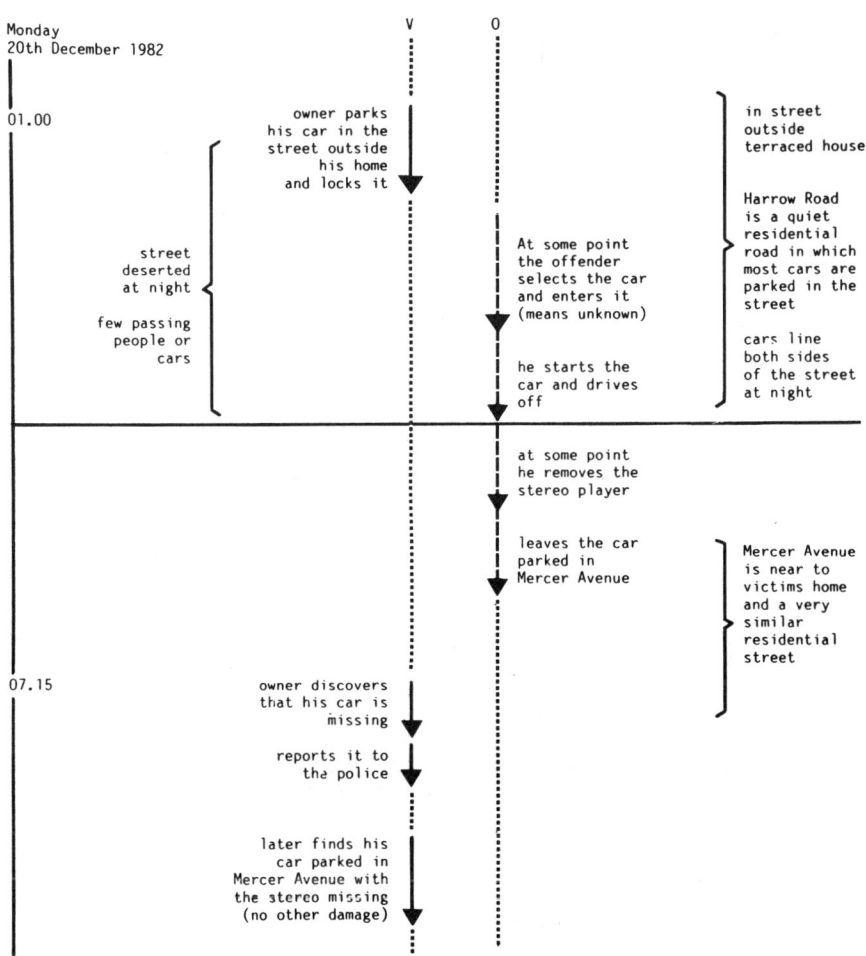

Monday
20th December 1982

V   0

01.00

owner parks
his car in the
street outside
his home
and locks it

in street
outside
terraced house

Harrow Road
is a quiet
residential
road in which
most cars are
parked in the
street

At some point
the offender
selects the car
and enters it
(means unknown)

street
deserted
at night

few passing
people or
cars

he starts the
car and drives
off

cars line
both sides
of the street
at night

at some point
he removes the
stereo player

leaves the car
parked in
Mercer Avenue

Mercer Avenue
is near to
victims home
and a very
similar
residential
street

07.15

owner discovers
that his car is
missing

reports it to
the police

later finds his
car parked in
Mercer Avenue with
the stereo missing
(no other damage)

V   Male, aged 30,   Harrow Road, Stanmore

0   Unknown

The stolen car was a green/black Ford Cortina Mk III reg no GKL 903M

Stereo player was valued at £50

Figure 3.4 A house burglary

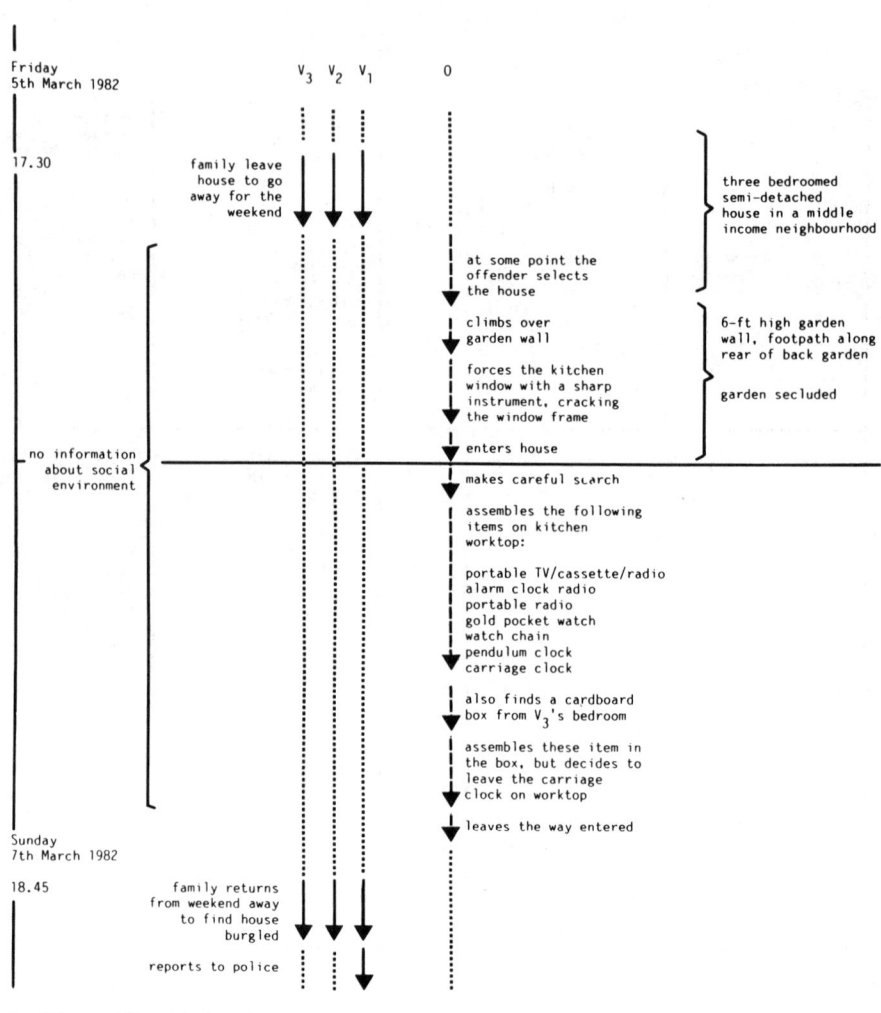

Friday
5th March 1982

V_3 V_2 V_1 0

17.30
family leave
house to go
away for the
weekend

at some point the
offender selects
the house

climbs over
garden wall

forces the kitchen
window with a sharp
instrument, cracking
the window frame

enters house

three bedroomed
semi-detached
house in a middle
income neighbourhood

6-ft high garden
wall, footpath along
rear of back garden

garden secluded

no information
about social
environment

makes careful search

assembles the following
items on kitchen
worktop:

portable TV/cassette/radio
alarm clock radio
portable radio
gold pocket watch
watch chain
pendulum clock
carriage clock

also finds a cardboard
box from V_3's bedroom

assembles these item in
the box, but decides to
leave the carriage
clock on worktop

leaves the way entered

Sunday
7th March 1982

18.45
family returns
from weekend away
to find house
burgled

reports to police

V_1 Male, aged 62, retired civil servant.   Cedar Avenue, Northampton

V_2 Female, wife of V_1

V_3 Male, son of V_1 and V_2

0   Unknown (digrams assumes only one offender)

Value of property stolen - final insurance claim amounted to £877.60

30

The diagram shows the process model of crimes in its general form. There is always and offender (0) and there may be several offenders involved in one incident who can be represented as $0_1, 0_2$.... Victims may not be directly involved with the offender but they take part in the sequence of events, if only to report the crime. They can be represented as V_1, V_2.... Others who may witness the crime or contribute something to the process can be represented as W_1, W_2.... What these actors do can be represented as a sequence of events (arrows) moving through time, the vertical dimension of the diagram. The physical and social environments can be described for each stage of the vertical process as Ep_1, Ep_2, Ep_3... and Es_1, Es_2, Es_3....

To illustrate how varied this form of presentation can be three examples are given of different kinds of crime. Figure 3.3 shows a case of a car stolen from outside the owner's house but found later by the owner with the stereo player removed. This is a typical example of a crime where there is little available information.

Figure 3.4 shows a burglary taken from a current study of residential crime, there is a little more information but still no contact with the offender.

Figure 3.5 shows an example from a study of street attacks in Coventry, where there was a direct and prolonged interaction between the victim and offender and so much more information about the incident (Poyner, 1980b).

The diagram can be taken on well beyond the point at which the critical event occurs, but beyond this point there would be no scope for preventive action because it would be too late to do anything to avoid the critical event – the crime has already happened. This point in the process has been labelled as the 'critical point' and is shown on all diagrams by a horizontal line. The main emphasis for research into crime prevention must be concentrated above the critical point, although it is often interesting and useful to continue the diagram beyond this point to record the outcome of the incident or the time it took for a crime to be discovered.

Crime sets

These diagrams do no more than record information about crimes that have already happened; they tell us nothing about prevention. It is only if there is a good chance that the same kind of crime will happen again that there is any justification for taking some preventive action.

It is possible to sort through a large sample of crimes and identify sets of very similar crimes. The more similar the crimes are within a set the more likely something can be done to prevent this kind of crime happening in the future. For example, if the same kind of crime happened regularly at the same place and at the same time of day everyday, it would be easy to deal with. However, even if crimes are not exactly repeated, sets of very similar cases can be regarded as potentially preventable if they are likely to recur in similar circumstances.

31

Figure 3.5   Drunk robbed on his way home

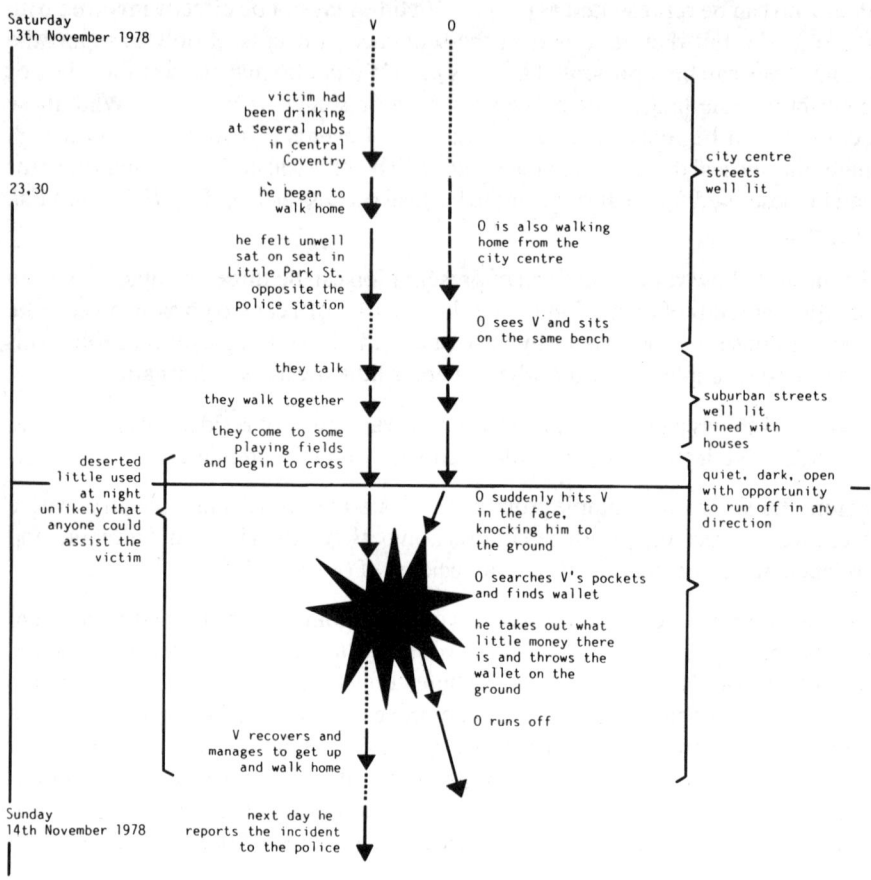

V   Male, aged 45, probably drunk, almost no money on him

O   Male about 25 years old, may have been drinking but not drunk

Loss/injury – V reported that £5 was missing; he also had bruising on his face

Two points are worth noting. If crimes cannot be grouped into sets of similar cases because they are different from other crimes then, at least theoretically, they should be regarded as unpreventable. Unless they are likely to be repeated in some way there is no point in giving thought to their prevention. Secondly, official crime categories in common use are far too crudely defined to be used to form crime sets. In practice, categories such as burglary, criminal damage, wounding and theft of motor vehicles encompass a wide range of diverse behaviour. Burglary might include cases where goods were stolen but there was no break-in, cases of break-in with nothing stolen or again cases of electricity meters being broken open but no sign of forced entry into the house. Each case is quite different.

32

In the kind of analysis being proposed here these types of burglary would be placed in quite different crime sets.

Although research is currently underway using this model, the most complete attempt to use the model in a crime study so far has been in a study of street attacks in the city centres of Birmingham and Coventry (Poyner, 1980b; 1983). Looking at those crimes which were originally classified by the police as robbery and theft from the person, the study found that most of these cases could be assembled into a number of quite specific crime sets. Examples of these sets include:

Robbery from street kiosks
Robbery of drunks
Money snatched while being taken to the bank
Handbag snatches
Purse/money snatched from hand after verbal ploy
Pickpocketing while boarding buses
Thefts from shopping bags

If we are successful in forming a set with a good number of very similar crimes, it is possible to summarise the whole set in much the same way as the individual cases are diagrammed. If we can imagine the idea of drawing out the diagrams for each incident on a separate transparent sheet so that they could be overlaid on top of each other, it would be possible to trace a general diagram that followed the form of all diagrams.

There is also a further advantage of this process of overlaying and combining incidents. In some cases we may have much less detail than other cases but otherwise the facts we do know about are the same. It may be possible to reconstruct the missing data in these less well reported incidents in much the same way as the archaeologist reconstructs broken pottery from an excavation. He may only have a few pieces of the broken pot but from knowledge of other similar pots he can be reasonably sure about the form of the whole pot. This archaeological approach is quite helpful when, for example, we may have some detailed accounts of what offenders do in a few cases where they have been caught. It seems reasonable to believe that similar behaviour occurred in similar crimes even though the offenders were not caught.

The best way to illustrate a crime set is to take one of those listed above which demonstrates particularly well how a crime set can be developed. Figure 3.6 summaries a set of incidents which involved pickpocketing at bus stops in the city centres. In the original study the set was formed of 31 incidents of which 30 were in the centre of Birmingham and one was in Coventry.

At first the concept for this set was to include any pickpocketing around bus stops, but as further incidents were read and recorded from the files, a much more specific type of crime emerged. For example, all victims were found to be middle aged or older men and they appeared to have lost wallets from the back pocket of their trousers. Observation of bus queues, where these incidents occurred, and the

33

general manner of dress of different aged groups at that time, suggested that this was the age group most likely to wear the kinds of trousers in which wallets are kept in a back pocket. Younger men tended to wear tighter fitting trousers and would keep money elsewhere on their person. Similarly women do not generally keep money in pockets and do not offer the right kind of target. Further observations of the queues where these pickpocketings took place, showed how long the queues were at rush hour (fig 3.6) and that it was possible to watch the queues from a distance. As intending passengers began to board the pay-as-you-enter buses, it was easy to pick out a likely victim. Each passenger had to reach into his or her pocket or handbag for money or a bus pass as they approached the entrance to the bus. We also realised that all the bus stops in question were sited on busy wide pavements

Figure 3.6   Pickpocketing at a city centre bus stop

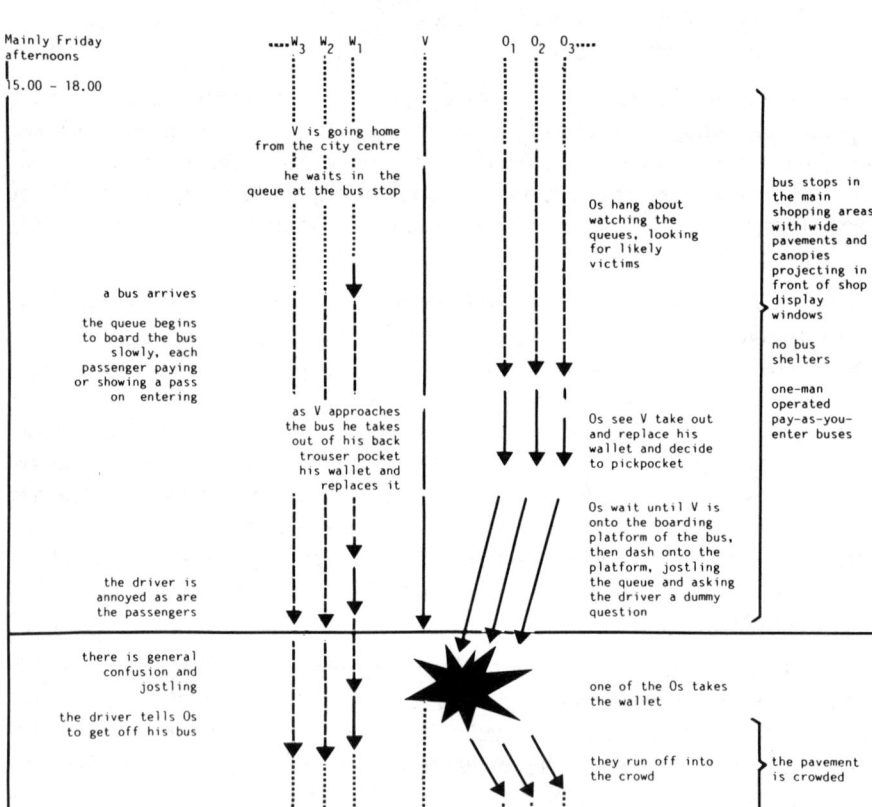

Mainly Friday afternoons

15.00 – 18.00

....W_3 W_2 W_1 V O_1 O_2 O_3....

V is going home from the city centre

he waits in the queue at the bus stop

Os hang about watching the queues, looking for likely victims

a bus arrives

the queue begins to board the bus slowly, each passenger paying or showing a pass on entering

bus stops in the main shopping areas with wide pavements and canopies projecting in front of shop display windows

no bus shelters

one-man operated pay-as-you-enter buses

as V approaches the bus he takes out of his back trouser pocket his wallet and replaces it

Os see V take out and replace his wallet and decide to pickpocket

Os wait until V is onto the boarding platform of the bus, then dash onto the platform, jostling the queue and asking the driver a dummy question

the driver is annoyed as are the passengers

there is general confusion and jostling

one of the Os takes the wallet

the driver tells Os to get off his bus

they run off into the crowd

the pavement is crowded

V   middle aged and older men – wearing trousers with back pockets in which they keep their wallets

O_1, O_2, O_3... small group of white youths

W_1 bus driver

W_2, W_3... other passengers in the queue

in front of department stores with display windows under wide projecting canopies – the perfect place for small groups of youths to hang about without raising any suspicions from those in the queues or from any passing police officer.

From the full set of incidents and our observations of the locations it was possible to piece together a very detailed description of this type of crime as shown in figure 3.6. During the afternoon rush period, particularly on Friday between 15.00 and 18.00 hours, groups of three or four youths would hang about near the main bus queues watching for suitable victims. As their victims began to board the bus, they would run up to the head of the queue on the boarding platform of the bus and jostle the queue. They would ask the driver some irrelevant question about the destination of the bus. Meanwhile one of the youths would pick the pocket of the victim. The victim would be irate at being jostled and would not realise that is pocket was being picked. The driver would shout at the youths to get off his bus and other passengers would be complaining. The youths would turn away and step off the bus and slip away into the crowd. The victim would not realise that his wallet was gone until later. None of the youths were ever caught.

Scope for prevention

If we look at the diagram of this crime set (figure 3.6), we can see that the statements above the critical point amount to a set of conditions that are necessary for this crime to occur. If we could make this model of the crime set perfect, the conditions defined in the diagram would be refined to the point where we could be confident that they were both necessary and sufficient for the crime to occur. In practice, it is difficult to be so scientifically precise about the definitions but it is an ideal to work towards. It may be possible with a very common type of crime, and with experience of dealing with it over time, that precise definitions can be developed.

If we assume that all the conditions above the critical point are both necessary and sufficient for the pickpocketing to occur, then we can see that it is possible, at least theoretically, to intervene in the situation at these bus stops by changing or re-designing some aspect of the system to prevent the pickpocketing taking place.

This implies that if we change any one or several of the conditions above the critical point the crime would not take place. For example, it would not take place if only women and young men were allowed to use the buses, or if the pavement was cleared of people except for people in bus queues. To propose these changes would be absurd because no one would accept them. However, there are ways of re-designing the situation at the bus stops which would be more acceptable. Here are four of the conditions in figure 3.6 which might be changed:

Payment on entry to the bus – During the afternoon rush period it might be possible to provide some alternative to 'pay-as-you-enter' at these city centre bus stops. Tickets might be sold to people in the queues before the buses arrive, or some other means of pre-purchasing tickets might be provided such as by machine.

Bus stops on wide pavements in front of shop display windows – Bus stops might be re-sited away from main pavements and organised in bays more like a bus station layout. This would make it much more difficult for the offenders to watch a queue from a distance.

The openness of the pavement around the bus stop – If the queues were less open to view and perhaps partially screened by a bus shelter or any other screening device, the offenders would be unable to watch the queues to see victims take out their wallets.

Direct access all round the boarding platform of the bus – This allows the offenders to dash onto the platform. They could not do this if some kind of queue marshalling barrier was constructed at the boarding point.

All these changes in the conditions of this crime set would probably eliminate pickpocketing at the bus stops. The question for those concerned with crime prevention is simply to decide which of the various methods to use, and indeed to decide if it is really worth using any of them. It will be primarily the responsibility of the bus operator to decide these questions, perhaps in consultation with the police and the city planners. It is unlikely that the bus operator will want to increase manpower and sell tickets manually at these bus stops, but the idea of some form of pre-purchase by machine might be attractive because it would also have the advantage of speeding up the movement of queues at the busiest time. The re-siting of bus stops is a more radical solution and would be very difficult to achieve in the centre of Birmingham which is already under great pressure for space for other public facilities; it would probably lead to less convenient locations for the bus stops. Perhaps the most practical possibilities are the idea of a screening bus shelter and the provision of a barrier to reduce access to the boarding platform.

When this bus stop example was first put forward, the bus stops in the centre of Birmingham had nothing but a pole to mark the stop (see figure 3.7). No doubt if the bus operator had been approached with the argument that a shelter or barrier should be built, there would be the usual cry of cost limitations. However, the operator did subsequently install a simpler shelter at these stops. Unfortunately, the design contributed nothing to the problem of pickpocketing as it does not screen the queue from the pavement. If the shelter had been of the same design as elsewhere in the city centre (figure 3.8) the evidence suggests that the pickpocketing would be stopped. No pickpocketing occured at bus stops with these shelters in the original study. It is also interesting that in the centre of Coventry, where the buses are run by the same operator, the stops in part of the central square do have barriers similar in design to figure 3.9. They were installed many years ago to reduce jaywalking when the square was a busy main route. The fact that no pickpocketing occured at these stops suggests that the barriers are effective. All this underlines the value of a carefully designed environment.

Figure 3.7   Bus stops: High Street, Birmingham

Figure 3.8   Bus stop with shelter

Figure 3.9   A marshalling barrier at a bus boarding point

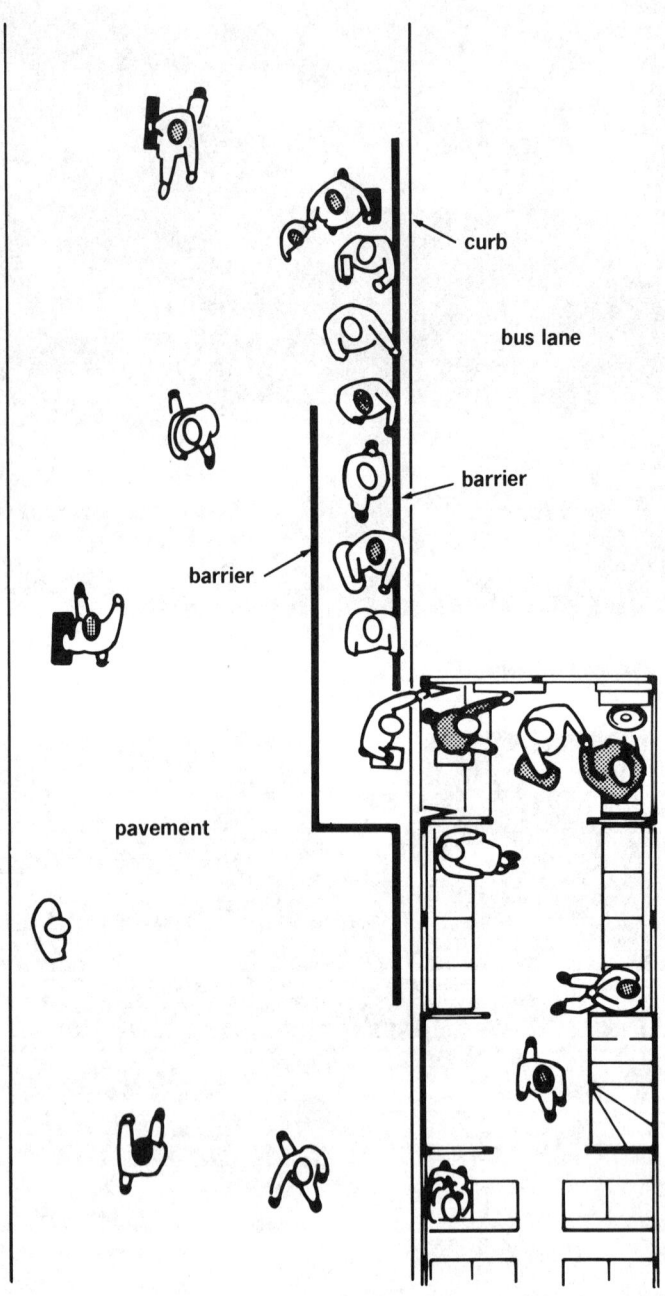

This process model of crime is continuing to provide the basis for a number of research studies and it will certainly evolve further. It is worth emphasising that one of the essential differences between this approach and the more conventional analyses of crime is the use of comparatively small categories of crime. This contrasts with the more familiar demands of statistical research methods for large samples and weighty evidence in favour of some preventive action.

What we find, however, is that it is well worthwhile trying to retain high quality in the definitions of crime sets, so that the incidents are really very similar. The more uniform or homogeneous a crime set can be made the more detail can be defined about the process and the conditions involved in the crime. As can be seen from their bus stop example, because the set is very uniform, it was possible to establish a good deal of description above the critical point which was common to all incidents in the set. The more that can be defined as necessary to the crime the more we can find options for prevention.

There is a simple principle here: the more uniform a set the greater the opportunity for preventive action. Even though we may be dealing with small numbers of incidents the method does seem to present a more reliable way of finding effective preventive measures. This may explain why so much preventive research has been disappointing. Because so much effort has been concentrated on crude groupings of crime types such as burglary, robbery or auto theft, it has been virtually impossible to find truly common facts about the conditions which lead to each of these groups of crime. The model implies that we have to be very patient and try to solve the problems of crime gradually and progressively, piece by piece.

4 Situational crime prevention from the offenders' perspective

Trevor Bennett

Over the last decade or so, the use of situational measures in the control of crime has increased markedly both in Britain and in the United States. The use of these measures is not, of course, new. Organised situational crime prevention can be traced back to 1829 when Sir Richard Mayne, one of the first joint commissioners of the new Metropolitan Police, specified that the primary object of the police was the prevention of crime; and he distinguished this from detection and punishment of offenders after crimes had been committed. What is striking is the growth of interest in situational methods and the new hope, especially noticeable among the police, that something might 'work' after all. Why has interest grown so rapidly in recent years? There are at least two explanations: first, the perceived limitations of existing crime prevention methods; and second, the development of new perspectives on the nature of criminal behaviour which are compatible with a situational approach.

The first explanation concerns the widespread (but not total) loss of faith in corrective methods which, in Britain, was reflected in the rapid change in direction of research conducted and funded by the Home Office Research and Planning Unit (HORPU). This is described in detail in Clarke and Cornish (1983) who report that the shift from 'social prevention' to 'situational prevention' in the HORPU was to a large extent a product of the failure of earlier research to generate realistic policy options. Their rejection of the treatment approach in the mid-1970s was based both on the discouraging findings of research on effectiveness (although they note that the results were not entirely negative) and on the inherent difficulty of manipulating 'social' factors to control crime. Situational factors, however, were more amenable to manipulation.

The second explanation concerns the development of new perspectives on criminal behaviour which had a common theme compatible with a situational approach. While it cannot be claimed that changes in theory caused changes in preventive methods, the availability of a supporting perspective made proposals for new initiatives more palatable to policy makers. The common theme of these theories was 'rationality' and 'choice'. Evidence of 'rational-choice' theorising can be found in psychology in 'subjective expectancy theory' (Edwards, 1954), 'interactive theory' (Cornish, 1978), 'decision theory' (Carroll, 1978) and the 'choice model' (Clarke, 1980); in sociology in the shift from 'positivist' to 'phenomenological' and 'radical' explanations of crime (Cicourel, 1968; Quinney, 1970); and in economics in the concept of 'limited rationality' (Cook, 1980). The rational-choice perspective provided a theoretical framework for the development of a situational approach to crime prevention.

It is clear, however, that the assumptions underlying situational measures go far beyond what has been discussed or hypothesised by academics in the disciplines mentioned above. They derive not from academic theory but from common-sense speculation or as Waller (1979) suggests "informed hunch". The theoretical basis of the approach, therefore, is a combination of beliefs which have not been articulated and hypotheses which have not been tested. The wisdom of embracing the situational approach as the future hope for crime prevention depends in part on the validity of the rational-choice perspectives and the specific beliefs on which it is based. This paper considers whether the theoretical underpinnings of the approach are justifiable by identifying underlying assumptions and by examining the perceptions and decision making of the types of offenders to whom these measures are directed.

What is situational crime prevention?

Before discussing the theoretical basis of the situational approach, it is necessary, in order to provide a framework for the discussion, to define what is meant by situational crime prevention and to describe the kinds of measures that are currently in use. The focus of attention throughout this paper is placed on the offence of burglary. Although situational measures are often designed to prevent street crimes and other household offences it is clear that the control of burglary is often a primary aim and sometimes the sole aim of these programmes.

Hough *et al.* (1980) define situational prevention as, "the use of measures directed at highly specific forms of crime which involve the management, design or manipulation of the immediate environment in which crimes occur in as systematic and permanent way as possible". It is sometimes referred to as "primary" prevention (Brantingham and Faust, 1976) or "opportunity reduction" (Gladstone, 1980). The kinds of methods used can be categorised under three main headings relating to the level at which they are designed to operate: (1) the individual; (2) the community; and (3) the physical environment.

Crime prevention initiatives aimed at the individual (e.g. the potential victim of burglary) are usually based on encouraging householders to make their homes more secure. These initiatives may be in the form of television campaigns or police-initiated publicity and leaflet campaigns which aim to persuade people to lock up their property or to fit additional security locks. Specialist crime prevention officers employed by all British police forces are available to give free security advice as a means of reducing residential crime. The recent innovation in property marking is another method aimed at the potential victim of burglary. In the United States this is often promoted under the heading of "Operation Identification" and involves citizens borrowing equipment from the local police department and marking items of value with an indelible identification number. In Britain, recent anti-burglary campaigns (e.g. the British Insurance Association's "Beat the Burglar" campaign) encourage property marking as do many of the police organised neighbourhood watch schemes.

The most common community-oriented crime prevention initiative in the United States, and increasingly so in Britain, is neighbourhood watch. Experiments with neighbourhood watch in Britain are now being conducted in more than half of the police forces and will soon be implemented by all police divisions in the Metropolitan Police District. The schemes in Britain operate along similar lines to those in America. People are invited to keep an eye on the houses of neighbours and to report suspicious incidents to the police. Watch campaigns usually form part of a comprehensive crime prevention programme which might include security surveys and, as noted above, property marking.

Crime prevention through environmental design has been most influenced by the ideas of Jacobs, (1961), Wood (1961), Angel (1968) and Newman (1972). In practice these programmes focus on improving street lighting, controlling access to buildings, restricting pedestrian and traffic flow and dividing grounds into identifiable areas. The most ambitious schemes have been conducted in America (see Fowler *et al.*, 1982), although the NACRO "area improvements" and "safe neighbourhood" projects involve some changes in environmental design (see Hedges *et al.*, 1980; Bright and Petterson, 1984).

Assumptions underlying the situational approach

Situational crime prevention is based on *general* assumptions about the way in which offenders think and act, and on *specific* beliefs about their perceptions and decision making at the time of contemplating particular offences. These assumptions and beliefs are not necessarily articulated, but they are implicit in the nature of the methods used. They derive from a combination of research findings, common-sense, informed hunch and speculation.

The key *general* assumption underlying the situational approach is that offenders freely and actively choose to commit crimes. The approach rejects the positivist view that offenders are in some way predisposed to commit crimes as a result of genetic, social or psychological factors operating in their past. Elements of the choice model have been described by Clarke (1980): "Some of the ... theoretical difficulties [of positivist explanations] can be avoided by conceiving of crime not in dispositional terms, but as being the outcome of immediate choices and decisions made by the offender." The assumption that offenders choose to offend and, perhaps more significant, choose not to offend, leads to at least two further assumptions about decision making.

First, the assumptions underlying situational crime prevention are based on the view that the decision to offend is made in response to the immediate circumstances and the immediate situation in which an offence is contemplated. Much less weight is given to the influence of past factors in the life history of the individual offender. This means that crimes might or might not be committed depending on situational constraints and inducements. The influence of situational factors on criminal behaviour have been noted by criminologists for some time (Lombroso, 1911; Ferri, 1895; Sutherland and Cressey, 1955). Little attempt was made to incorporate these observations into a general statement about the nature of criminal behaviour. More recently, however, writers have attempted to develop a situational perspective on crime (Briar and Piliavin, 1965; Gibbons, 1971; Ohlin, 1971).

Second, the situational approach is based on the view that the motivation to offend is not constant nor beyond control. The motivation to offend is seen as dependent on the calculation of costs and rewards rather than the result of inheriting or acquiring a disposition to offend. If the motivation to offend was uncontrollable, then crimes prevented would merely be displaced. Reppetto (1976), for example, argues that situational prevention is based on the assumption that the motivation to offend is neither constant nor determined and concludes from his own study that: "... even if one is prepared to concede the primacy of individual motivation in determining criminal behaviour, one must acknowledge that motivation is not constant for all offenders at all times and that mechanical prevention programs may, in fact, absolutely prevent a certain amount of crime".

The *specific* assumptions underlying situational crime prevention vary from programme to programme. In order to examine these beliefs, it is necessary to look at each measure individually.

Initiatives aimed at the individual include, as described earlier, fitting and using security hardware (e.g. locks and bolts); fitting and using detection hardware (e.g. alarms); and property marking. McInnes *et al.* (1982) identified two assumptions underlying campaigns which encourage the use of security hardware: the first is that potential offenders will not possess the skills or tools necessary to overcome the device; the second is that (if they do possess the necessary skills or tools) they will perceive the time required to overcome the device as an unacceptable risk. Mayhew (1984) suggests that the target hardening approach to preventing residential burglary rests on the premise that burglary is "invited" by lax security. It is believed, she argues, that the bulk of burglars perceive security as a "crucial deterrent" – an idea which "remains tenaciously at the centre of much preventive policy".

Crime prevention publicity campaigns rarely offer an explanation of why householders should fit burglar alarms – stating no more than that they increase the "security" of the home (see *Crime Prevention News,* 1982). The aim of "silent" alarms which are connected directly to the local police station is clearly to catch offenders after the offence has been committed. Alarms which are neither linked to the police nor silent presumably are intended to scare off intruders before entry is fully affected or before goods have been stolen. (It is also possible that an alarm might serve to signal that an offence has taken place which might reduce both reporting and police response times.) Campaigns aimed at promoting greater use of burglar alarms as a means of deterring burglars are based, therefore, on the assumption that offenders perceive the existence of an alarm, or an activated alarm, as an unacceptable risk. Whereas the function of security hardware is to obstruct (and possibly to deter) entry, the function of detection hardware is largely to alter offenders' perceptions of the probability of getting caught.

44

The stated aims of property marking are more diverse. Duncan (1980) specifies four ways in which identifying property might affect levels of burglary. First, it is assumed that burglars will perceive the theft of marked property as too risky because it can easily be traced. Second, law enforcement officials will be able to prove that items in the possession of a suspected burglar are stolen. Third, recovered items can be claimed and returned to their legal owner. Fourth, the transfer of stolen property from the burglar to the fence will be made more difficult.

The assumptions about criminal behaviour underlying community based programmes are not at all clear. Some reports suggest that neighbourhood watch campaigns aim to catch offenders after crimes have been committed (i.e. there are not necessarily any assumptions about offenders' perceptions or decision making). McInnes et al. (1982), for example, note that neighbourhood watch programmes operate as an "adjunct to the protection offered by the police". Other reports indicate that assumptions about criminal behaviour are implicit in neighbourhood watch schemes.

In the publicity material relating to the programme implemented by the Cheshire police it was stated that its aims were to encourage participants to keep watch on unoccupied dwellings and to collect mail, remove newspapers and cut grass to give empty dwellings the appearance of being occupied. Collecting mail and making unoccupied buildings appear occupied are not methods of catching more offenders, but are attempts to reduce perceived opportunities for crime. Comments such as these suggest that neighbourhood watch has, in fact, dual aims. Evidence of this can be found in an Assistant Commissioner's memorandum on neighbourhood watch schemes operating in London. The basic idea behind neighbourhood watch, it is noted, is for the community to become the "eyes and ears of the police" and to reduce opportunities for criminal activity. The former of these aims need not involve any assumptions about criminal behaviour (although it might be believed that offenders are deterred from attacking communities which are organised to become the "eyes and ears of the police"). The latter of these aims does involve assumptions about criminal behaviour: namely that burglars are deterred by occupants, signs of occupancy and the presence of neighbours.

The principles underlying crime prevention through environmental design are more clearly elaborated in the literature. Many of these measures have been influenced by Newman's concept of defensible space (1972). The two main components of the defensible space concept are "territoriality" – dividing grounds and buildings into "zones of influence" and "surveillance" – designing buildings which allow easy observation. The aim of generating territoriality is to motivate residents to defend their own areas by encouraging informal social controls. This is intended both to catch more offenders and to deter them by increasing their perceived probability of getting caught. The assumption underlying surveillance is that it facilitates the observation and reporting of suspicious incidents to the police. Again, this is intended both to catch offenders and to deter them.

The way in which offenders perceive territoriality and surveillance is not specified by Newman. Some writers believe that there should be more research into offenders' perceptions of different kinds of buildings and areas in order to draw out the assumptions underlying the notion of defensible space (Mawby, 1979). Mayhew (1979) notes that there are many basic questions that need to be answered concerning the perceptions of offenders: do they feel more vulnerable in defended areas and (if so) do they fear being seen by residents or do they have other fears?

The offender study

In this chapter the validity of some of the general and specific assumptions underlying situational prevention will be considered by drawing on the findings of a research project conducted between 1979 and 1982 on the perceptions and decision making of convicted burglars. The main method used, which involved the largest sample of offenders and occupied the major proportion of the research time, was a semi-structured interview. Its advantage over other methods is that it allows subjects to speak freely and at length using their own concepts and terminology. As the interviews can be tape-recorded and transcribed verbatim, respondents' methods of describing and explaining their behaviour can be preserved. As offenders were required to discuss quite difficult and complex issues, it was important that the method of interviewing chosen should allow them the time to express themselves as clearly and fully as possible.

In addition to the semi-structured interview, the research included three experiments on different samples of offenders. The aim of these experiments was to reveal the kinds of situational cues that were used by burglars in their assessment of dwellings as potential targets for burglary. In order to ensure that offenders identified and commented on situational factors that they, rather than the researcher, thought were relevant, it was necessary to use visual rather than verbal stimuli.

The first method comprised a video-recording of thirty-six dwellings, including eight blocks of three or four neighbouring houses and one block of three flats. The recording was made by filming from a van travelling along the road at approximately walking pace. Our intention was to simulate what offenders might have observed if they were walking along the same route. The second method involved showing respondents photographs of dwellings in order to examine the relative importance of certain visual cues. Offenders were shown a photograph of the front of a dwelling only. They were then asked to request further photographs until they had sufficient information to make a decision to commit or not to commit the offence. The third experiment involved showing burglars photographs of different aspects of five dwellings. Two sets of photographs were produced: the first showing the houses in a favourable state (as hypothesised from a burglar's point of view) in terms of five control variables (whether alarmed, or whether there were signs of occupancy, window locks, cover and the presence of neighbours); the second set of photographs showed the houses in an unfavourable state. Each offender saw a combination of houses in favourable and unfavourable states and was asked whether he would consider them as suitable targets for burglary.

The majority of offenders were selected systematically from the files of a number of prisons and borstals situated in the southern half of England. The remainder were selected from local probation departments with the assistance of probation officers. In total, 309 offenders were used at some stage of the research: 128 participated in the semi-structured interview, 51 were given a structured interview and 130 took part in one of the three experimental methods. Inevitably, the samples were not identical, although they were sufficiently similar to make them comparable. Overall, the majority of offenders were aged twenty-one years or over and admitted more than fifty burglaries in their lifetime. As there are no reliable estimates of the characteristics of unconvicted offenders, it is difficult to know to what extent the samples are representative of all burglars. It seems likely, however, that the samples over-represent older and more experienced burglars. A fuller account of the characteristics of offenders can be found in Bennett and Wright (1984).

Offenders' perceptions and decision-making

The key *general* assumptions underlying situational prevention are: (1) the decision to offend is to some extent situationally determined; and (2) the motivation to offend is not beyond control.

In order to assess the validity of the former proposition, we asked offenders who took part in the semi-structured interview to describe the way in which the decision to commit a burglary was typically arrived at during their last period of offending. The analysis of their responses revealed that the vast majority of offenders identified some kind of precipitating factor or trigger which prompted their decision to offend. The responses fell into six main categories. In order of importance, these were: (1) the influence of instrumental needs; (2) the influence of others; (3) the influence of presented opportunities; (4) no precipitating factor; (5) the influence of expressive needs; and (6) the influence of alcohol. Details of these responses have been published elsewhere and need not be repeated here (see Bennett and Wright, 1984).

What, then, do offenders' accounts tell us about whether the decision to offend is situationally determined? The amount of support given depends on the way in which both the "decision to offend" and "situational determinants" are defined.

A "situational factor" can be defined in a limited sense as a temptation or inducement to crime – in other words, as an opportunity. This definition matches most closely the common-sense concept of an opportunistic crime whereby an offender, who is thinking about other things, discovers by chance an opportunity for burglary which precipitates a desire to offend. Interpreted in this way, our research offers little support for the first proposition. The vast majority of offenders interviewed said that they usually decided to offend before the target had been selected.

47

Alternatively, the term "situational factor" can be defined to include a wide range of conditions which might influence the decision to offend. These might be physical or non-physical and might exist at the time and place of the contemplated offence or at other times and places. For example, an offence might not be committed if the offender fails to meet an accomplice, if he is unable to obtain suitable transport or if he is side-tracked by other events. On the other hand, an offence might be committed if the offender is coaxed or goaded by others, if he is intoxicated or if he is pressurised by financial need to commit crime. Such factors were identified by the early proponents of the situational perspective as likely influences on the decision to offend. Erez (1979), for example, speaks not only of physical determinants, but also of social and cultural ones. Briar and Piliavin (1965) noted the influence of "conflicts", "opportunities", "pressures" and "temptations" on criminal behaviour.

The "decision to offend" is also an ambiguous term. Offences are rarely committed as a result of just one decision, but involve many decisions which are made between the original motivation to offend and the final decision to commit an offence against a particular target. Whether or not the decision to offend is considered as situationally determined depends also on which decision is being referred to. It has already been suggested that the original decision, the motivation to offend, is seldom influenced by physical situational factors, although it is frequently influenced by social, cultural and economic factors. The final decision to commit an offence against a particular target, however, is likely to be influenced by physical situational factors. The difference between the two is exemplified in the case of an offender who decides, for example, to commit an offence as a result of a need for money, but refrains from doing so because of an excessive police presence in the area of the proposed offence.

Which of these interpretations is most relevant in assessing the validity of the situational approach? Burglary prevention programmes currently focus on two broad approaches: the first aims to reduce the number of situational temptations in an attempt to reduce the chance of motivating the unmotivated; the second aims to alter the decision-making calculus at the scene of potential crimes in order to discourage those already motivated from fulfilling their desires. Situational prevention is directed, therefore, towards situational factors narrowly defined as physical opportunities and towards the final decision to offend. Our research findings suggest that there are two combinations of definitions of situational factors and the decision to offend which are best supported by the accounts of offenders: the assumption that physical opportunities affect the final decision to offend (which is the focus of some preventive measures) and the assumption that social, cultural and economic facts affect the original decision to offend (conditions which are rarely the subject of situational prevention). The belief that physical opportunities affect the original decision (an assumption also implicit in preventive programmes) was not supported by our findings (in relation to the types of offender sampled).

48

The second general assumption is that the motivation to offend is not uncontrollable. In other words, it is assumed that offenders who have been prevented from committing an offence against a particular target will not simply be "displaced" and commit another offence against another target or return to the original target at another time. In order to examine whether offenders ever change their minds about offending, it is necessary to operationalise the concept of displacement. Displacement, like deterrence, is essentially a psychological process; to determine whether a person is deterred or displaced we need to know what he or she was thinking about at the time of the offence. Strictly speaking, an offence is displaced if an offender's specific intention to commit an offence is eventually carried out, either in relation to the original choice or target or another target. If the intention is not carried out and the offender refrains from offending the offence is not displaced. This would be so even if the offender committed a similar offence soon afterwards, so long as it related to a different intention. It would have been methodologically unsound to ask offenders to distinguish retrospectively between offences committed in response to different intentions. The problem of operationalising the concept of displacement was simplified, therefore, by making the assumption that the motivation to commit an offence related to one day only. It was assumed that if an offender refrained from committing an offence and the offender did not commit another offence that day, the intention to offend had been suppressed and the offence had not been displaced. If an offender refrained from committing an offence but committed a similar offence the same day, the offence had been displaced. In order to examine the extent to which burglars changed their minds about offending, they were asked to tell us what they normally did if something put them off committing a burglary.

About forty per cent of the sample said that if they were put-off an offence, they would usually commit another offence during the same day and about another forty per cent said that they would not attempt another offence that day. The remainder reported that their behaviour depended on circumstances. Offenders who typically planned their offences were more likely than those who searched for suitable targets and committed offences there and then to report that they would not seek out another target that day.

If offender motivation was uncontrollable, it would be expected that once the decision to offend had been made that the offence would inevitably be committed. In fact, over half of the burglars who described their behaviour after being prevented from committing an offence said that they either "usually" or "sometimes" gave up and went home. There is some support, therefore, for the assumption that the motivation to offend is capable of being suppressed. It should be noted, however, that many of the offenders who said that they would not attempt another offence that day said that they would do so within the next few days or weeks. Whether this should be regarded as displacement would depend on whether the decision to offend related to the intentions formed at the time of the original offence.

The main "specific" beliefs about criminal behaviour concern the deterrent or pre-

49

ventive effectiveness of certain measures and the way in which they alter perceptions and decision making. To what extent do these beliefs concur with offenders' accounts?

The main thrust of initiatives aimed at the potential victim of burglary has been in relation to security hardware (locks and bolts). Although locks and levels of security were noted by burglars, they were not mentioned very frequently and they were not described as being particularly influential determinants in their final decision to offend. The use of detection hardware (e.g. burglar alarms) are less frequently emphasised in crime prevention campaigns, although out findings suggested that burglar alarms were avoided by a large proportion of offenders. Other kinds of detection hardware (e.g. cameras) and property marking techniques were not discussed with offenders. In addition to these more common initiatives, there are other situational factors that are capable of being manipulated by individual householders, although they rarely feature in crime prevention campaigns. Signs of occupancy, for example, were often mentioned by burglars yet are seldom mentioned by crime prevention officers.

Community-based initiatives are currently dominated by neighbourhood watch or block watch campaigns. The findings of most relevance to these projects is that burglars often said that they tried to avoid being seen by neighbours. They were most concerned, however, with the immediately adjacent neighbours rather than with people further away. A discouraging finding for some community-based projects is that many of our offenders seemed unconcerned about passers-by or police patrols, arguing instead that it was necessary only to wait until the people had passed before approaching the target.

What do offenders' accounts tell us about methods which seek to reduce crime through environmental design? Some offenders said that they generally avoided choosing houses that abutted busy roads and others reported that they were concerned about the level of surveillability. This usually related to the extent to which a potential target was overlooked by the windows of nearby buildings. More often, however, the offenders said that they were concerned about the presence and proximity of buildings immediately at the front, back and sides of the property. A number of other factors relating to building design and management were mentioned by offenders, although these feature very little in burglary prevention programmes. One of the most important factors identified by burglars was the amount of cover surrounding a dwelling. Open-plan estates were often cited as being too risky because of the increased chance of being seen entering the property. Another important factor relating to building design was the availability of rear access. The focus of crime prevention through environmental design on factors relating to surveillability and territoriality has perhaps drawn attention away from environmental factors associated with the *immediate* situation of potential targets.

Implications for situational crime prevention

The evidence of the offender study gives some support to the assumptions under-lying the situational approach. The project has identified certain areas, however, in which these assumptions are less well supported.

Offenders' descriptions and explanations of typical offences indicate that the var-ious decisions to offend (initial, intermediary and final) are made consciously and deliberately. They also suggest that these decisions are often influenced by events and circumstances bound up in particular situations. A decision to offend made in one situation may be overturned by events and circumstances in another. The research offers support, therefore, for the major principles of the rational-choice model proposed by Cornish and Clarke (see Chapter 1) and also the underlying assumption of situational crime prevention that decisions to offend are influenced by situational factors and that these decisions are potentially changeable. This general conclusion, however, requires qualification.

There are many types of situational factor and there are many decisions that are made between the motivation to offend and the offence. Situational crime preven-tion measures are typically based on manipulating *physical* opportunities for crime in order to affect both the *initial* decision to offend (by reducing opportunities which might motivate the unmotivated) and the *final* decision (by altering the balance of costs and rewards at the scene of potential crimes to discourage those already motivated). On balance, it would appear that (in relation to the type of offenders interviewed) there would be more mileage in manipulating physical opportunities in order to influence the *final* decision to offend. Very few offenders said that they were motivated by the chance discovery of opportunities for burglary. The major drawback of aiming to prevent crimes after the offender has decided to commit an offence is that the motivation might not be controlled and offences prevented might be displaced. Although these two types of measure are not incompatible, it makes sense to focus preventive efforts on (potentially) the most rather than the least effective methods.

What about other possible combinations of types of situational factors to be man-ipulated and stages in the decision-making process? Manipulating social, economic or cultural situational factors in an attempt to influence either the initial or final decision to offend are less practicable options. The research findings suggest that the initial decision to offend was usually precipitated by perceived economic need or by the influence of others. One preventive option is to pay offenders not to offend or, more realistically, to pay them to perform community work (see Guardian, 1983). Whether this would be sufficient to meet their finan-cial needs or socially acceptable during a period of high national unemployment is unlikely. Manipulating social factors also seems impracticable. As many offen-ders said that the initial decision to commit a burglary was made in conversations with others in pubs or while drinking, a conceivable option is to control public drinking or the sale of alcoholic drinks. Such changes, however, would affect both offenders and non-offenders alike and are unlikely to be generally acceptable.

Few preventive options flow from the knowledge that social, economic and cultural factors sometimes influence the final decision to offend. The problem is either that they cannot be manipulated or that they cannot be manipulated without major changes that would adversely affect the general public and individual liberties. Overall, therefore, the current level of operation of situational measures is probably as far as is practicable to go.

Offenders' accounts of their perceptions of specific situational cues, however, suggest that changes could be made in the types of methods used. The research showed that the *final* decision to offend or not to offend was most influenced by cues relating to the risk of getting caught. Cues relating to the potential rewards of the offence or to the ease or difficulty of entry were mentioned much less often. The most important risk factors concerned "surveillability", "signs of occupancy" and "presence of neighbours".

A great deal of the accumulated research evidence supports the conclusion that the key situational cues used by burglars relate to surveillability and signs of occupancy (there is little evidence on the impact of neighbours). Studies by Waller and Okihiro (1978), Winchester and Jackson (1982) and Reppetto (1974) all noted differences in occupancy patterns between householders of victimised and non-victimised dwellings. Research based on interviews with burglars also has demonstrated the importance of occupancy in offender decision-making (Walsh, 1980, Maguire and Bennett, 1982).

It is surprising that cues relating to surveillability and occupancy have not featured more prominently in burglary prevention programmes. In England, one of the most frequently employed burglary prevention programmes is the security campaign.

The Home Office Crime Prevention Centre at Stafford has relied heavily on encouraging residential security as a means of combating residential burglary. Crime prevention officers almost invariably advise householders to fit additional security locks. Future burglary prevention programmes need to be based on what is known about offenders' decision-making. Burglars rarely mentioned social cohesion, police response times, area access, citizen or police patrols, pedestrian movements or traffic flow as important factors in their decision-making (factors central to some community and environmental design and management programmes). This is not to say that these factors do not have some effect on offenders' choice of target (Allatt, 1984; Maguire and Bennett, 1983, Mayhew, 1984). Nevertheless, it makes little sense to under-emphasise the use of measures which might have the greatest preventive impact.

What kinds of programme aim to manipulate the factors noted by offenders as important in their decision-making? One method which includes a great deal of what the burglars mentioned is "neighbourhood watch". Many of the programmes initiated in the United States included attempts to increase the surveillability of properties and to create signs of occupancy (Cirel *et al.,* 1977). It is notable, however, that many of the neighbourhood schemes recently implemented in Britain (particularly in London) have left out the creation of signs of occupancy. However, they all included attempts to involve neighbours in the protection of their own and others' properties and, apart from the occupants themselves, burglars reported that neighbours were the next important group of people to avoid.

Concluding comment

Like any single piece of research, the offenders study has managed only to scratch the surface of the many issues involved in the study of offender decision-making. It must also be remembered that the burglars who took part in the research represented the older and more experienced offender and the results might not be generalisable. Nevertheless, the research has demonstrated that the study of offenders is a potentially fruitful approach which might lead not only to a fuller understanding of criminal thought processes, but also to the development and design of rational situational measures. In order to manipulate offenders' decision-making it is preferable to first understand it. The current level of knowledge on the subject so far has demanded that programmes be implemented on the basis of speculation. It is perhaps surprising that the assumptions underlying the approach match the reports of offenders as well as they do.

5 Property marking as a deterrent to domestic burglary

Gloria Laycock

Marking property to indicate ownership is not new. Mattick *et al* (1974), in a brief history of "possession marking", begins with a description of the personalised symbols on the bone tools of Palaeolithic man about 25,000 years ago, and goes on to list many other examples throughout history of the marking of possessions. There thus appears to be a long established belief that the branding or labelling of property with a personal symbol will in some way protect it from theft or ensure its return should it be lost. In recent years the practice has been given fresh impetus in the United Kingdom in consequence of two developments – first, the development of the post code – in combination with the house name or number, this provides a unique, and publicly available identifier of the household to which goods belong. And secondly, acceptance by the police that they will routinely examine property recovered for signs of ownership, paying particular attention to the possibility that the article may be post coded.

Building upon these developments many police forces are promoting property marking as a crime preventive device. Although the practice appeals to common sense, there has been little effort within the United Kingdom to marshal firm evidence of its effect on domestic burglary. In this paper some of the recent evidence from North America and Sweden will be briefly reviewed and the results of an evaluation of property marking presented and discussed in terms of effects on crime and police/public relations. The results will be considered in the light of current theoretical issues.

Results of previous research
A nationwide study in the United States of a range of 'operation identification' (O-I) projects was carried out by Heller and his colleagues (1975). He identified several goals in relation to these projects – burglary deterrence (here a distinction was drawn between deterrence on a city-wide basis or only for those participating in the schemes); an increase in the recovery and return of stolen property; an increase in the difficulty of disposing of stolen goods and an increase in the detection of offences or prosecution of offenders.

Heller's conclusions can be summarised as follows:

(i) participants had significantly lower burglary rates after joining than before (O-I projects in Seattle and St Louis reported reductions of 33% and 25% respectively);

(ii) cities with O-I projects did not enjoy city-wide reductions in burglary rates;

(iii) the presence of markings did not significantly hamper the disposal of stolen property;

(iv) there was no evidence to suggest an increase in either the apprehension or conviction of burglars; and

(v) there was no evidence that O-I markings appreciably increased either the recovery or return of stolen property.

Heller also identified a range of practical difficulties associated with the initiatives – public participation rates were low, recruitment costs per household were considered high and initiatives were difficult to maintain.

The most recent study of operation identification was carried out by the National Council for Crime Prevention in Sweden (Knutsson, 1984). This particularly comprehensive project covered a residential area about 20 miles from Stockholm; it contained about 3,500 houses, in the main detached but including some terraced property, and a small number of flats. Over a four-year period the participation rate in the scheme rose from about 13% to just under 30%. This made evaluation difficult but working on the basis of a number of well argued assumptions the author concluded that the programme had not led to a reduction in burglaries even for those participating in the schemes.

Knutsson also reported on interviews with burglars which indicated that the majority of burglars would take little notice of a sign indicating that property was marked. This is a particularly important finding since it suggests that marking property would not lead to a reduction in burglary rates even for those displaying stickers, and is contrary to the evidence from the United States. However, there were a number of difficulties with this aspect of the study. The sample size was extremely small; it was drawn from a different area (Stockholm itself); the burglars had all been caught and, although it is not made particularly clear in the report of the study, all seemed fairly experienced as burglars. For these reasons its seems advisable to treat the conclusions from this part of the work with some caution.

On balance the research evidence does not provide substantial support for investment in property marking as a deterrent to burglary. At best the North American experience indicates a reduced rate of victimisation for those participating but there has always remained a sufficiently large pool of unprotected homes and as a result overall burglary rates have remained unchanged. Furthermore, it has never been clear from any of the research why the participants should enjoy reduced burglary rates. There is no evidence that goods are more difficult to fence; that burglars are more likely to be arrested; that potential offenders are aware of the signs and symbols associated with participation or that goods are likely to be returned.

The South Wales scheme

Despite these essentially negative conclusions British police forces have recently been launching property marking with enthusiasm. The Metropolitan Police, to take an example, spent £242,000 in 1983/84, and £30,000 in 1984/85 on publicity around the capital recommending the marking of property as a crime preventive device with a further £90,000 on equipment. It was decided therefore that a demonstration project on property marking should be carried out in the United Kingdom. The conditions for the launch of this scheme were to be optimal on the grounds that if there were no reduction in burglary rates under such conditions then there would be little point in pursuing property marking nationwide.

The primary aim of the scheme was to reduce the chances of burglary for those participating. In view of this it is obvious that it is not the marking of the goods which is important but the extent to which it is *advertised* that the goods are marked. It was stressed throughout the project, therefore, that the single most important factor was the window or door sticker which had to be displayed. It was assumed that the sticker would convey not only the message that goods are marked and disposal may be difficult, but also, and in practice more significantly, that the residents in this house are concerned about burglary and that the risks to the potential offender may thereby be increased. In addition, insofar as property marking might be expected to protect property rather than cash, it was decided to concentrate the evaluation on those burglaries resulting in the loss of markable goods.

Because of the manner in which the scheme was launched, it was expected that there might be an improvement in police/public relations and an attempt was made to assess this as part of the study. Finally, a record was to be kept of goods returned as a consequence of marking, although with little expectation of an impact.

A high take-up rate by residents in the target area was regarded as crucial to the scheme. This was in order to make statistical analysis possible and to reduce the pool of unprotected homes thus, hopefully, limiting the opportunity for the displacement of burglary. Three methods were employed to achieve this – the scheme was launched with as much publicity as possible; door-to-door visits were made by the police or special constables, and free marking equipment and door or window stickers were provided for the residents.

To expand upon these three methods. Prior to the launch a letter was sent to all residents by the Chief Constable, alerting them to the impending event. The launch itself, on 17 November 1983, was marked by a press conference attended by, amongst others, the Chief Constable and Home Office officials. Local television coverage was also obtained. For the following three days the force crime prevention officers together with the special constables under their direction, visited the houses in the target area. There were ten teams of officers working in the area over Thursday, Friday, Saturday and Sunday. A weekend was included to ensure that more people would be at home; the officers also worked during the evenings.

In order to ensure some uniformity of approach the force crime prevention officers, who led each team, attended an afternoon seminar some weeks before the launch. At this seminar the aims of the scheme were outlined and any anticipated difficulties resolved. A short training session was also organised for regular beat officers and special constables.

The scheme was explained on the visits to homes in the area by the police, free equipment was provided and help offered in marking goods to any elderly or infirm members of the public. The officers also completed a brief questionnaire on which they recorded the name and approximate age of the person with whom they had spoken, whether or not they agreed to participate in the scheme or whether or not the equipment had been left with the householder. One call-back visit was made if the occupants were not at home on the first visit.

Stylus pens and stickers were provided free of charge by the Post Office; Berol Ltd., provided ultra-violet pens for the invisible marking of property. This sponsorship, together with the use of special constables, enabled the scheme to be launched with minimal costs.

One week following the initial visit all those participating in the scheme were revisited by the police or special constables. A further questionnaire was completed recording which goods were marked, whether any difficulties were encountered (help was offered if necessary), and whether, and if so where, the 'property marked' label had been placed (e.g. front door, back window).

After three months had elapsed a further letter was sent to residents from the Chief Constable reinforcing the aims of the scheme and enclosing another window/door sticker. Finally, in order to check on the extent to which interest continued to be maintained a further visit to those participating was carried out on 24 June 1984, approximately six months after the initial launch. A record was made of the number of houses still displaying the sticker and an extract from *Crime Prevention News* (1984), in which the scheme was described, was provided for those participating. Further stickers were provided where necessary.

The target area
The area chosen was part of the Caerphilly sub-division of the South Wales Constabulary. Three fairly distinct 'villages' were included which covered the floor of the valley. Low lying and largely uninhabited hills defined the area which limited the opportunity for displacement. Burglaries were not uniformly distributed throughout the villages. They were concentrated on a group of local authority homes which fell more or less in the middle of the valley. Thus any displacement of burglary from the initially higher risk area would be likely to fall on one of the other two villages within the scheme. A plan of the area is shown at figure 5.1

The three 'villages', Trethomas, Graig-y-Rhacca and Machen can be described loosely as follows –

Trethomas – a mixed area of detached, owner-occupied accommodation together

Figure 5.1   Map of the research area

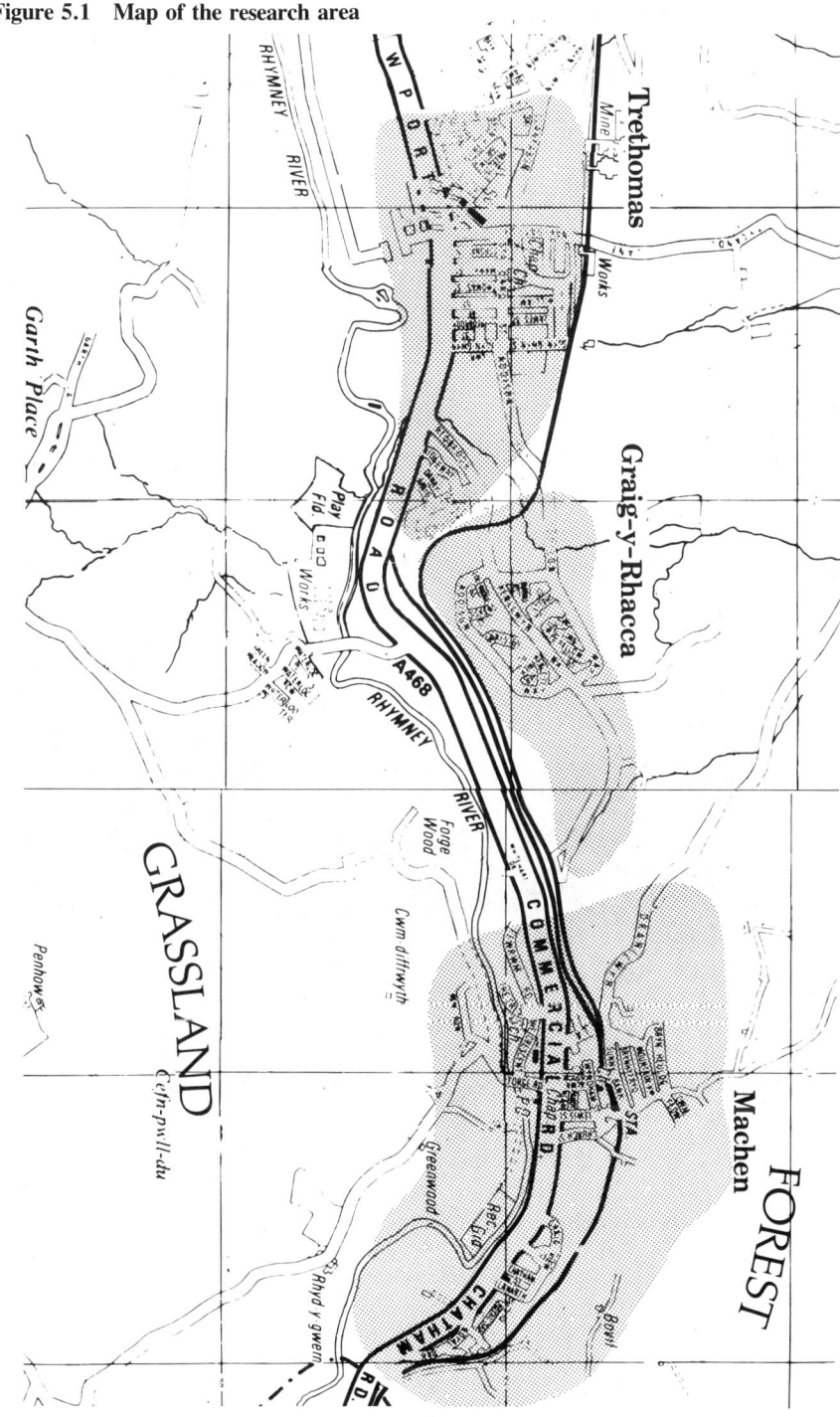

with an area of older 'mining' houses once owned by the coal board but now either local authority owned or owner occupied. These houses are mainly back-to-back terraced. There are approximately 800 dwellings in this total area.

Figure 5.2   A street in Trethomas

Graig-y-Rhacca – an area of local authority housing arranged as maisonettes or terraced houses. The estate is rather untidy in places although some houses are well cared for and of good decorative order. There are approximately 700 homes on this estate.

Machen – an area of largely privately owned accommodation with gardens, garages, *etc.* Some houses are local authority owned but are less 'estate-like' than those in Graig-y-Rhacca. Some of the outlying houses back onto picturesque woodland. There are approximately 700 houses in this area.

Figure 5.3   Graig-y-Rhacca Estate

Figure 5.4   Machen

The evaluation

Criteria employed

A dwelling was considered in the target area if it appeared on the electoral register and was part of the sub-division area outlined in figure 5.1. A total of 2,234 houses were thus included in the target sample.

A house was considered to have been burgled if it appeared in the police list of 'reported burglaries'.

A household was regarded as IN the scheme if, following the second police visit, a 'property marked' sticker was on display on any outside door or window. Otherwise it was regarded as a non-participating household.

The scheme was launched by the Chief Constable on 17 November 1983. Reported burglaries for the 12-month period from 1 November 1982 to 30 October 1983 were recorded as the 'BEFORE' period; from 1 December 1983 to 31 November 1984 as the 'AFTER' period. Data from the month of November 1983 were excluded from the evaluation.

Methodological issues

(i) Sample size and displacement

Applied research calls for compromise and the present initiative is no exception to this general rule. Whilst in principle a large sample of target households would have been preferred, in practice, due to constraints of cost, the sample size had to be limited. In addition, because the resources required to investigate displacement would have been prohibitive, an area was chosen which naturally restricted the geographic displacement opportunities for burglary.

(ii) Data on burglaries

The main aim of the initiative was to reduce burglary which raised the possibility of a 'dark figure' of unreported burglaries in evaluating the scheme. If the dark figure were known to remain a constant proportion of committed burglaries then it could have reasonably been ignored. But there are common-sense grounds for suggesting that when a community has attention drawn to crime, through the launch of an initiative of the kind proposed, then burglaries which were formerly unreported might be reported following the initiative, thus producing an apparent rise in offending. The standard response to this possibility is to carry out a crime survey of the area before and after the launch of the scheme. However, again for reasons of cost, this was not possible. It was estimated, however, using unpublished data from the first British Crime Survey (Hough and Mayhew, 1983), that if the evaluation were to be carried out in terms of changes in the loss of markable goods (excluding jewellery which was expected to be difficult to mark in any case), then the potential increase in offending (due to an increase in the number of unreported burglaries being reported) would be minimal. As an additional check, the police asked householders on their first visit, whether or not they had been burgled during the previous 12 months. This procedure is less than ideal since there may be some reluctance to admit an unreported burglary to a police officer. Nevertheless, it was felt to be a useful check. This exercise revealed 19 incidents in the year prior to the launch of the scheme. This was fewer than might have been anticipated from the results reported in the British Crime Survey. These incidents were disregarded in the analysis.

The data on crime was thus provided by the police. This practice has been criticised for its accuracy, reliability and validity on grounds other than those related to the unreporting of crime (see for example, Burrows and Tarling, 1982; Farrington and Dowds, 1985). Such criticism reinforce the argument for using victims' surveys which, for reasons of cost, was not possible. Some safeguards, however, were taken. For example, the police officers whose responsibility it was to launch the scheme, oversee the visits to homes in the area and obtain the funding, were from the force Crime Prevention Department and based at Police Headquarters; those responsible for sending burglary data to the Home Office were based on the Sub-Division concerned. They sent information directly to the researchers and had limited contact, if any, with those police officers with a particular interest in the scheme. Furthermore, if the police were to be selective in forwarding reported burglaries, it is most likely that they would fail to mention those incidents in which there was no loss. There were seven 'nil taken' burglaries before the launch and a comparable number – nine – during the follow-up period.

(iii) Assessing police/public relations

A similar difficulty arose in relation to assessing the effect of the scheme on police/public relations. Whilst ideally it would have been preferable to carry out a house-to-house survey before and after the scheme this was not possible. As a compromise the police asked, on their second visit to those participating, whether they had any general comments. The police themselves were also asked for an assessment of their reception by the community when calling at houses.

Results

The take-up rate

The participation rate for households in the three areas is shown in Table 5.1. Those excluded from the scheme include households in which there was nobody at home or which were unoccupied at the time of the visit, those who declined to join, and those who, although agreeing to join the scheme, declined to display the sticker.

Table 5.1: Participation rate by area.

Area	In scheme	Out of scheme	Total	Take-up rate
Trethomas	618	203	821	75%
Graig-y-Rhacca	499	209	708	70%
Machen	497	208	705	70%
TOTAL	1,614	620	2,234	72%

Of the non-participants 185 had joined the scheme, in the sense that they had claimed to mark their property, but had declined to use the window sticker and were thus counted as non-participants. In almost all cases their reluctance was because they felt that they would be *more* likely to attract a burglar if they did so. Interestingly, the incidence of the non-user of stickers appeared in small clusters in the data – i.e. it seemed as though neighbours had discussed whether or not to place the stickers in the window and had decided as a group not to do so. Thus there might be a small street or group of houses where the stickers were not displayed but where the response to the scheme was otherwise positive.

Each participant was asked which goods they had marked. The majority reported marking electrical goods – televisions, videos, radios, music centres and other domestic equipment such as cookers and washing machines. Only 4% marked jewellery which is understandable given the difficulty of doing so and also went some way toward supporting the decision that jewellery should not be considered "markable" from the point of view of the evaluation.

Householders were asked whether they had any difficulty with the marking equipment. Difficulties were expressed in a very few cases with marking clothes or jewellery but in general comments were almost all favourable. It is of course possible that the positive comments resulted from the fact that the pens were provided free of charge – it may have seemed ungracious to complain about the performance of a free gift!

If a property marking scheme is to be launched in an area, it is important to know whether or not the public are familiar with their post code. In the course of the initial police visits participants were asked whether or not they knew the post code; if they did not, the police officers were able to provide it. It transpired that 30% of those who agreed to participate did not know the post code. On the local authority housing estate, where burglaries were most common and thus where property marking was most relevant, 40% of householders did not know their post code.

Burglaries before and after the launch

In the 12-month period before the launch of the scheme there were 128 burglaries reported to the police. In the 12-month period after the launch 74 burglaries were reported – a reduction of 40%. The effect of the scheme on the *rate* at which homes were victimised sounds rather less dramatic of course. Allowing for the fact that some houses were burgled more than once, the burglary rate before the launch was 5.1% and after was 3%. This reduction was statistically significant.

The burglaries were not uniformly spread across the area. Although the victimisation rates for Machen and Trethomas were similar that for Graig-y-Rhacca was considerably higher. The figures are given in Table 5.2 below with Machen and Trethomas data combined.

Table 5.2: Burglary rates before and after the launch of the scheme by area

Area	Before Number of houses burgled at least once	Rate	After Number of houses burgled at least once	Rate
Machen and Trethomas	23	1.5%	15	0.98%
Graig-y-Rhacca	92	13.0%	53	7.5%
Total	115	5.1%	68	3.0%

The data in Table 5.2 show statistically significant reductions in victimisation rate in Machen/Trethomas, Graig-y-Rhacca and the valley as a whole following the launch of the scheme.

In order to determine whether the property marking scheme was relevant to these reductions in burglary rate, comparisons were made between those participating in the scheme and those not participating. The results of these comparisons are shown in Table 5.3. The table records incidents of burglary rather than houses burgled – in other words if a house was burgled on more than one occasion it is counted more than once – the figures are not therefore strictly comparable to those in Table 5.2 above.

Table 5.3: Burglary incidents for participants and non-participants before and after the launch of the scheme

	Before	After	
Participants	91	35	$(p<0.001)$
Non-participants	37	39	(no significant change)

The table shows a reduction in the number of burglary incidents for those participating in the scheme. Whilst there was no reduction for the non-participants there was also no significant increase in incidents – i.e. there was no displacement of burglary from one group to another.

One of the expectations in setting up this scheme was that if it had any effect on burglary rates this would be through its impact on the loss of goods which were markable. It was assumed that a burglar might be deterred from committing an offence by a 'property marked' sign only if he had been 'in the market' for television sets *etc.*, – i.e. goods which might be marked. The effect on those potential offenders on the look-out for cash was expected to be marginal. In order to investigate these effects the burglary incidents were examined in more detail. Burglaries were divided into those in which 'markable' goods were stolen, those involving the loss of cash from pre-payment fuel meters and 'others' (see Laycock, 1985), for a list of the kind of goods considered 'markable').

Approximately 25% of the reported burglaries in the 12 months before the scheme was launched related to the loss of cash from pre-payment fuel meters. These meters are offered by the gas or electricity companies as an alternative to quarterly or monthly billing to those households which experience difficulty in budgeting. Such householders are often on low incomes and prefer the advantages which pre-payment metering can offer. A considerable disadvantage to this system is that large sums of money, perhaps over £100, may accumulate awaiting collection by the fuel companies. The meters thus provide an attractive target to the would-be thief. Pre-payment meters are more common on local authority housing estates such as Graig-y-Rhacca. Because of this the data in Table 5.4 (below) distinguishes between Graig-y-Rhacca and Machen/Trethomas.

Considering first the Machen/Trethomas area, the data indicate that a significant reduction in the loss of markable goods was achieved for those participating in the scheme; there was effectively no change for the non-participants. There was no change in relation to either loss from meters or other burglaries for either those in or out of the scheme although it should be noted that the numbers involved are exceedingly small. In Graig-y-Rhacca, where the base burglary rate was higher, there was a significant reduction in the loss of markable goods for those participating ($p<0.05$) but also a significant reduction in the number of meter breaks for those in the scheme ($p<0.005$) and in the number of 'other' burglaries ($p<0.025$). There were no significant changes in relation to the victimisation of non-participants in Graig-y-Rhacca.

Table 5.4: Type of burglary before and after the introduction of the property marking scheme

Type of burglary		Before	After
		Machen/Trethomas	
Markable property	in scheme	10	0
	out of scheme	3	5
Meter breaks	in scheme	2	1
	out of scheme	0	2
Other burglary	in scheme	6	6
	out of scheme	4	2
		Graig-y-Rhacca	
Markable property	in scheme	21	11
	out of scheme	12	11
Meter breaks	in scheme	30	9
	out of scheme	8	14
Other burglary	in scheme	20	7
	out of scheme	16	11

The data presented in Table 5.4 are not comparable with those data in earlier tables because of multiple counting from any one incident – e.g. if a burglary involved both the loss of cash and of goods then it is counted twice.

The return of stolen goods and the detection of offenders
No goods were returned to the public as a consequence of the operation of the

scheme. This is not as disappointing as it may seem however because of the goods stolen from participants only two television sets and two hi-fi units were reported as having actually been marked.

Twenty-one offences were reported by the police as having been detected following the launch of the scheme but there is no evidence to suggest that the operation of the property marking project played any part in these detections. Certainly no marked goods were recovered from those charged.

The cost of the initiative
Estimating the financial costs of crime prevention initiatives, with the implication that if they are judged to be too expensive they will be stopped, is a dangerous path down which to travel. It is difficult to take account of the reduction in distress caused to burglary victims or in the reduction in costs to the criminal justice system of processing potential offenders who may have been put off committing offences by the scheme. These savings can be considerable (see, for example, Lipsey, 1984) but there are obvious difficulties in attempting to attach a value to them.

In addition there are general expectations on the part of the public that the police will provide a service almost irrespective of the cost – the investigation of murder provides an extreme example but a great deal of the more mundane police work has inherent 'social' consequences. It is often easier to overlook these factors than to try to estimate their effect when setting out on cost-benefit exercises.

Despite this caveat, it is clear that there should be some financial monitoring of all police work and crime prevention is no exception. The present initiative cost £847 in police overtime, £650 in mileage allowance and £470 subsistence – a total of £1,967. The cost of deploying the special constables, who are unsalaried, was £168 in meal allowances and £605 mileage allowance. The total extra cost to the force was thus £2,740.

In the first year of operation there were 54 fewer burglaries than in the previous year. Estimating the cost in police time at about £40 per burglary[1], we have a cash saving of £2,160 pounds. If there are 15 or more fewer burglaries than before the initiative was launched in the second year of operation then the scheme will have broken even or be in profit in cash terms.

On balance, bearing in mind the effect on police/public relations described in the next section and the other unquantifiable advantages outlined above, the initiative can fairly be described as 'cost effective.'

The effect on police/public relations
In the absence of social surveys it is difficult to draw firm conclusions on the effect of this initiative on police/public contacts. Nevertheless, a take-up rate of over 70% must be seen as an achievement and reflects well on the persuasive and positive approach adopted by the police officers involved. The police, in

---

[1] These estimates are approximate and based on figures from Burrows (1985) and Crust (1975).

reporting back after the launch of the scheme, spoke of a welcoming reception by the public and the comments which they collected from participating households were almost without exception complementary.

One of the difficulties in attributing the positive attitude of the public to the launch of the scheme is that the householders in the area may have always felt positive toward the police. And in the privately owned, middle class homes of Machen this may well have been the case. However this was almost certainly not the case in Graig-y-Rhacca where the burglary rate was relatively high and where the police felt that a large number of local offenders lived. There was some anxiety felt by certain of the police officers in going onto the estate on a door-to-door basis and the anticipated reaction from the householders was one of aggression. It therefore came as a surprise to find that the take-up rate on the council estate was as high as anywhere else in the valley and that the reception from the public was warm. It is with rather more confidence that the good relations between the police and public might be attributed to the launch of the initiative in this area than in the others.

Discussion
The demonstration project described in this chapter was set up in a carefully chosen area. There is difficulty, therefore, in generalising the results to other less ideal areas. But the study can be justified on the grounds that if property marking had not reduced burglary here then it is doubtful whether it could do so anywhere.

The study addressed similar issues to those raised in the earlier work in the United States and in Sweden. In some areas different results have been obtained. There is a need to explain – the high take-up rate; the reduced burglary for those participating in the scheme and the valley-wide reduction in burglary. These, and other issues, are discussed below.

The take-up rate
The take-up rate of this scheme was almost twice as high as that achieved elsewhere. There are three factors of immediate significance. First the considerable advance publicity given to the scheme in the locality, secondly the door-to-door approach by the police and finally the provision of free marking equipment. It is not possible to determine which of these three factors were of greatest significance but the fact that the police were prepared to visit every home and to follow-up this with a further visit one week later must have played an important part in convincing the public of the worth of the exercise.

A more general point in relation to the high take-up rate is that whatever the public were being asked to do in protecting themselves against burglary had to be made as effortless as possible on their part; this was a guiding principle in the design of this scheme. It was helped greatly by the existence of the post code and the efforts by the post office to extend its use. In other property marking schemes which have been launched, particularly in the United States, householders have been required to register their personal code with the police or lodge with them a list of items marked with the appropriate marking recorded. This clearly requires far more effort on the part of the individual members of the public. The existence of a nationally available post code in the United Kingdom offered as considerable advantage.

Looking in detail at the take-up rate along the valley, and bearing in mind that the householders are from different social classes and live in remarkably different property, there was a notable similarity in take-up rate in the three 'villages'. It is particularly remarkable that a high participation rate was achieved on the council estate; the area which had the highest rate of burglary. The police were themselves surprised at the positive reception they received in this area because it has a rather 'rough' reputation and, they felt, housed some so-called problem families.

In retrospect it is obvious that nobody likes to be the victim of a burglary, not even a burglar, and for the ordinary (non-burglar) members of the public on the estate who were at greater risk than elsewhere, there was clearly good reason to join the scheme.

Reduced burglary for participants
The observed reduction in victimisation rate (38%) for those participating in the scheme is higher than was reported from the United States and clearly greater than was obtained in Sweden.

Looking in detail at the results obtained, in the lower burglary rate areas of Machen and Trethomas the impact of the scheme was upon the loss of markable goods, which suggests that property marking *per se* was the significant factor. But in the higher rate area of Graig-y-Rhacca there was also a significant reduction in 'meter break' burglaries and 'other' burglaries. The results here stem, surely, not in marking of the property but in the message to potential burglars that the risk of breaking into this home is greater than that associated with another 'unmarked' home; the residents here, so the message reads, are concerned about burglary and the risk of capture is therefore greater. If this is a correct analysis of the situation, then any 'burglar beware' label would have been equally effective in this part of the experimental area provided that the potential burglar believed that his risks were increased. In this area the present initiative seems to have been as much as evaluation of the effect of a label *saying* that property was marked as of the effect of marking property. The difference between these two statements has not been fully explored in other studies and merits further investigation in the future.

The question remains, however, as to why the effect of the label was different in the different areas. One reason for the difference stems from the unexpected reduction in the number of burglaries involving the loss of cash from pre-payment meters. Indeed, the greatest reduction in any category of incidents was in relation to meter breaks in Graig-y-Rhacca. This is, on the face of it, an odd result. But there is evidence, both anecdotal and empirical, that many of the reported burglaries involving the loss of cash from pre-payment fuel meters are not 'real' burglaries but result from householders 'doing their own meter'. Estimates of the extent to which this occurs vary considerably but it could be the case that as many as 80% of reported burglaries involving the loss of cash from pre-payment meters are 'own-goals' (Hotson, 1969). That being so, the explanation of the drop in meter breaks in Graig-y-Rhacca is more easily explained, not as a real reduction in burglary, but as a reduction in the number of individuals taking cash from their own meter. They were persuaded by the police to join a burglary prevention scheme and subsequently realised that in joining they had unwittingly debarred themselves from claiming to have been burgled. This effect stems, perhaps, from the increased risk to the householder, rather than the burglar, who anticipates police interest should he claim to have been burgled following a meter break. It would be interesting to know, if this analysis is correct, what was the effect on the domestic economy as a result. There are, according to police officers, two major reasons for 'own goals'. First the householder decides that the money in the meter is still 'sort of theirs' and since they have run out of cash for food or whatever, they may as well 'borrow' it back. In these cases it might seem reasonable to assume that the householder will borrow the money from a friend, or do without, if they feel they can no longer borrow from the meter. The second source of 'own goals' is not the householder but another member of the household. In some of the most crime prone areas in the north of England police officers suggest that money is often taken from meters in order that the adolescents in the household can buy drugs. In these cases it might be assumed that there would be implications for the displacement of crime.

Displacement of burglary

One of the major differences between the results reported here and those from other studies is that there was no apparent displacement in burglary from participants to non participants. The most plausible explanation for this seems to relate to the exceptionally high take-up rate achieved by the police. Or the approximately 30% 'unprotected' houses a number would perhaps be less likely to be burgled for other reasons, for example, they may have a burglar alarm or be particularly visible from the surrounding area. This would have the effect of reducing the pool of potential targets still further. As Cornish and Clarke emphasise in their chapter, the displacement of crime is a crucial issue for crime prevention. The results reported here might be seen as encouraging the belief that displacement effects can be overcome, but it remains an empirical question to determine at what level of participation displacement ceases to occur. In addition, no evidence is presented here on displacement to other crimes although there have been no reports from the police of a marked increase in street crime or robbery in the area.

In other studies it has never been so clear that in persuading the public to mark their property the police were at the same time persuading the potential burglars that the scheme would be effective. Bearing in mind the original distribution of burglary throughout the valley it is almost certainly the case that the police, in calling at almost every door as they did, were also calling at the doors of the burglars. It seems plausible that this contributed to the apparent lack of displacement. The manner in which the scheme was launched raised the profile of prevention to a remarkable extent; it involved considerable media coverage and a great deal of police activity, none of which can have gone unnoticed by the local burglars.

Return of goods and the capture of offenders
The conclusion that the goods were not more likely to be returned is quite compatible with other studies. Nor is this at all a suprising finding. Although it is no doubt the case that the police recover vast quantities of goods, presumed stolen, in any year, it is also the case that those goods are a very small proportion of the total stolen. In order for property marking to make significant reductions in the Aladdin's caves of the urban police forces, a substantial proportion of the general public would need to mark their goods. This raises the question as to the appropriate degree of emphasis to give the practice of marking property on these grounds. Furthermore, there is some evidence, albeit anecdotal, that the public would rather not have returned their worn out television set when the insurance company has paid up for a new one! Unfortunately, it is probably the items of sentimental value, old jewellery and the like, which the public would like to see returned, but which is the most difficult to mark.

Another of the arguments in favour of property marking is that offenders are more likely to be caught or convicted. Again there was no evidence from this study to support this view. There are, nevertheless, instances from other areas where goods have been returned or where offenders have been caught. Although such instances seem sufficiently rare to cast doubt on the extent to which the marking of property would act as a deterrent to the professional and sophisticated burglar, they may be sufficient to deter the young, opportunistic offender who is in the majority.

Conclusions
The results of this project suggest that property marking can reduce the incidence of domestic burglary. But there are a number of reasons why this may not be replicated elsewhere so easily. It seems likely that the success depended upon the high take-up rate achieved and upon the fact that the local burglars, or would-be burglars, knew as much about the operation of the scheme as did the ordinary householders.

The study points to the complexity of the phenomenon of domestic burglary and illustrates how even an apparently simple strategy of marking the goods can have operate in a number of ways at several levels. In order to tease out these various effects detailed information needs to be collected from a variety of sources. This is particularly the case if displacement is to be understood and the critics of situational crime prevention are to be answered.

6 School design and burglary

Tim Hope

This chapter reports a research study which examined the link between the design of schools and their vulnerability to burglary (see also Hope, 1982; 1985). It set out to determine whether situational design features associated with school buildings could account for the variation in rates of burglary between individual schools. The chapter first reports the findings of this study and then draws some specific recommendations for reducing the risk of burglary in schools. It concludes with a broader assessment of the implications which this study has for situational crime prevention.

The sample consisted of 59 separate school sites within the Inner London Education Authority (ILEA). There seemed merit in concentrating effort where burglary was most prevalent. Consequently, the study focused on single-sex boys' and co-educational secondary schools which had the highest rates of burglary amongst ILEA schools. All the schools were regarded as having a mixed ability or 'comprehensive' intake of pupils. The research was based on an analysis of ILEA records, interviews with head teachers and caretakers, and site surveys, and gave information on: the characteristics of burglary; the areas in which the schools were located; the design of school buildings; and certain aspects of their management. Between 1976 and 1978 these 59 school sites suffered 430 burglaries between them. As with other forms of burglary, relatively few persons are convicted of burglaries to schools and it was not feasible to discover who breaks into schools nor what their motives might be. Head teachers and caretakers, however, were able to describe what they regarded as typical burglaries to their schools. According to them, the most common type of burglary was more a 'nuisance' than anything else. It was thought that these usually involved local adolescents who were familiar with the school layout. Little of value was stolen during these incidents unless it happened to be lying around; there may have been some damage but rarely anything serious. Less common, in their view, but still comprising a substantial number, were what might be thought of as 'professional' burglaries; where a concerted and planned attempt was made to steal expensive audio and visual equipment. Schools did not seem to suffer very often from 'malicious' burglaries involving substantial vandalism and serious incidents of arson also seemed rather rare. Some corroboration of these impressions was obtained from ILEA records. Just under half the burglaries during the three year period involved the theft of equipment whose replacement value was £25 or less (at 1978 prices). Nevertheless, 30 per cent of burglaries involved equipment which cost £100 or more to replace. It was, however, impractical to quantify from ILEA records the damage caused during burglaries. Most burglaries occurred late at night, many at weekends.

73

Although school burglaries seem fairly trivial for the most part, they nevertheless represent a breach in the security of school buildings which might at some time turn into something more serious. What is also worrying is that some schools suffer far more from burglary that others. In this sample, a quarter of the schools accounted for over half of all the burglaries, while half the schools produced no more than a tenth of the total number of burglaries. The next step therefore was to see why this was so; and especially whether schools with markedly different rates of burglary also differed in their design or location.

The effect of school design
Details of the design of schools were derived from site plans for each school supplemented by direct observation by the author. Some 13 variables were used to characterise the overall design character of individual schools, which reflected its size, layout and the character of its buildings and grounds. These variables accounted for a sizeable proportion of the variation in burglary rates between schools ($R = .48$; $p.<.001$). Preliminary analyses found that they were highly inter-related and it was decided to form them into a simple scale to express the overall design character of each school (Hope, 1982).

Table 6.1 Design attributes associated with schools high or low on the design continuum scale.

	Schools low on Scale	Schools high on Scale
1. Area of buildings	small	large
2. Area of site	small	large
3. Number of buildings	few	many
4. Concentration of buildings	concentrated	diffuse
5. Compactness of buildings	compact	sprawling
6. Height of tallest building	'low-rise'	'high-rise'
7. Proportion of single storey structures	none	some
8. Amount of glazing	little	substantial
9. Age of buildings	old	modern
10. Buildings of different ages	same age	different ages
11. Density of buildings to site	dense	sparse
12. Proportion of site under grass	none	mostly grass
13. Whether 'landscaped'	none	trees, flowerbeds etc.

Note
All descriptions are relative to the maxima and minima of the attributes within the sample measured.

To understand this scale it is helpful to contrast two types of school which might be found at either end of this design spectrum (Table 6.1). Schools located towards the lower values of the scale were small, compact schools mostly built before 1920. Their buildings were concentrated on restricted sites devoid of grass, trees and shrubs. They tended to be brick-built and not have substantial areas of glazing. They can be conveniently described by the abbreviation SOC (short for 'small, old and compact'). Many of these schools are typical of the classic 'Board School'

74

design (Seaborne and Lowe, 1977). At the other end of the spectrum can be found large, post-1945 or remodelled schools. Their somewhat 'sprawling' buildings were set in extensive grounds which were often grassed and landscaped. Their buildings varied substantially in height and often contained large areas of glazing. For convenience, these will be termed LMS schools (short for 'large, modern and sprawling').

The design of schools – as expressed by the design scale – was significantly related to the frequency of burglary (r. = .53; p. .001). A detailed examination of Table 6.2 helps to illustrate the differences in burglary rates between different types of school. Although schools at the SOC end of the design scale had significantly fewer burglaries than other schools, as schools more closely resemble the LMS design tendency, differences in burglary rates become much more variable. While LMS-type schools had the highest rates on average, the range of variation was much greater – some, in fact, had rates similar to SOC schools. There are therefore problems: first, why SOC schools should have uniformly low rates of burglary; and second, why certain (predominantly LMS) schools should suffer markedly different rates of burglary although they are of similar design.

Table 6.2   Frequency of burglaries in different groups of schools within the design continuum, 1977–1978

	SOC schools (low on design continuum) (n. 20)	Schools intermediate on design continuum (n. 19)	LMS schools (high on design continuum (n. 20)	Total schools (n. 59)
Number of schools burgled:				
10–24 times	–	4	7	11
5–9 times	1	3	6	10
1–4 times	12	10	5	27
Number of schools not burgled	7	2	2	11
Average number of burglaries per school	1.4	5.1	7.9	4.9
Index of variation in burglaries within groups (variance)	2.2	23.9	42.2	29.3

Differences in burglary rates between schools could not be accounted for by differences in areas in which schools were located nor the characteristics of their pupil intake; although these factors increased the probability of burglary in combination with design. In addition, although LMS schools had greater numbers of pupils than SOC schools, their generally higher rates of burglary seemed due to differences in design rather than, perhaps, to a greater number of potential offenders. It therefore seems that a school of an SOC design is not attractive to burglars.

One explanation might be that a small, compact school provides a beneficial atmosphere, discouraging the growth of anti-school sentiments amongst its pupils.

There is a body of evidence suggesting that schools which create a sense of involvement amongst their pupils suffer less crime (National Institute of Education, 1978), have less misbehaviour during the school day (Rutter *et al.*, 1979) and have fewer pupils who become involved in delinquency (Reynolds and Jones, 1978). It could be that SOC schools provide an 'ecological setting' (cf. Barker and Gump, 1964) which enables beneficial staff/pupil relations to develop naturally, while only some larger schools manage to overcome the deleterious effects of size. Unfortunately, the data in this study were insufficient to test this hypothesis.

There is, however, another explanation of the absence of burglary at SOC schools; they may provide fewer *opportunities* for burglary. There are perhaps three broad types of opportunity for burglary in schools: opportunities for access to premises; opportunities to commit burglaries without being seen (surveillance); and the availability of property to be stolen. SOC type schools appeared to offer fewer opportunities for burglary than other schools. First, they seemed less accessible. They more often had: high, brick-built perimeters; heavy wooden sash windows protected by grills; robust external doors and few opportunities to gain access to roofs. Second, they seemed to afford greater opportunities for surveillance. They were situated in areas of greater population density, and in less suburban areas. They tended to be close to public thoroughfares and their perimeters consequently benefited from ample street lighting. Because they had simple compact layouts, less of their building exterior was hidden from view and it was in any case better illuminated by lights which were fixed directly to building exteriors. All this suggests that people living in the vicinity of schools, along with resident caretakers, had good opportunities for surveillance. These schools may also have had less equipment available to be stolen since they were more likely to have fewer pupils and were more often part of split-site schools. They may therefore be less attractive to 'professional' burglars.

On all three counts – access, surveillance and the availability of equipment – LMS schools generally seem to be more conducive to burglary. They were situated in quiet, suburban neighbourhoods away from main roads and the size of their buildings and grounds probably meant that, once inside, burglars could operate without fear of being seen. Size also meant that there were a greater number of secluded and easily accessible places of entry in LMS schools compared to SOC schools. Since they had a larger number of pupils and were more likely to be used for a variety of purposes in the evening, they were more likely to have valuable property available for theft. Nearly all schools had some evening use, but a greater amount of use at LMS schools seemed not to deter the burglars, probably because burglaries tended to occur late at night.

Differences between schools of similar design
Although LMS schools had more burglaries than SOC schools, some schools (mostly, but not all, towards the LMS end of the spectrum) had considerably more burglaries than others with similar designs. What are the reasons for this? Part of the reason may be that these schools had even greater opportunities for burglary

than others. Those 'non-SOC' schools with high burglary rates offered greater opportunities for access to roof areas (and consequently a greater total amount of access opportunities) and were less open to informal surveillance from the caretaker's house.

There is also some suggestion that 'school factors' might reduce the vulnerability of some non-SOC schools. A greater number of these schools were voluntary-aided, fewer of their children came from broken homes and fewer lived near their schools. It would however be necessary to mount further research to explain these findings. One possible explanation might be whether their pupils identified more closely with them, either because of parental support, a denominational connection or through efforts by the schools themselves. Alternatively, these schools, paradoxically, may be less accessible and familiar to the surrounding community. Not only were their pupils more likely to live outside the immediate area, but the schools were also much less likely to host local authority youth centres and adult education institutes. Although they were used just as frequently in the evenings as other schools, their activities were more private or school-based.

Policy implications
The design of schools seems to have a significant influence on the number of burglaries they suffer. This raises three possibilities for prevention: building schools to different designs; changing educational policies; or seeking piecemeal environmental improvements to existing schools. There seems little prospect of reducing school burglaries by building different schools since it is likely that the projected decline in the school-age pupulation for some years to come will be met by taking the older, smaller schools out of commission, with relatively little new school building (Department of Education and Science, 1977). Nevertheless, in the future it may be possible for architects when designing or remodelling schools to take opportunities for access and surveillance into account. Although there have been some encouraging developments in this direction (e.g. Zeisel, 1976; Greater London Council/ILEA, 1977) more 'development' work is undoubtedly needed. Changing the way schools are run in order to reduce burglary seems hampered by the absence of a reliable empirical basis for intervention. Much of the evidence to date is scant or equivocal. Moreover, research into the relationship between educational approaches and misbehaviour in schools is difficult to mount and may require substantial time and effort (cf. Rutter et al., 1979). Nevertheless, changes can and do occur in the way schools are run and it would be instructive in the future to see whether such changes had any influence on the rate at which schools suffered from crime.

More promising, at least in the short term, are piecemeal environmental improvements to schools. What seems sensible is a more strategic approach to burglary prevention. Here, this research may have helped in drawing attention to the most vulnerable schools where most effort is needed. For example, there seems little need to improve the security of SOC type schools (although existing arrangements ought to be maintained) and attention might usefully be turned to LMS type schools. Three improvements arising from this research seem worth exploring. First, a case could probably be made for additional night-time surveillance at the most vulnerable schools. Although all schools in the study had a resident caretaker, the scale and design of LMS type schools may reduce their deterrent effect, since it seems much more difficult in these schools for a caretaker to be aware of night-time intruders who might be on the premises. Second, the lighting of LMS school sites could be improved to increase the surveillance of the premises by caretakers and passers-by, and to scare off intruders. Finally, gains could probably be had from improving 'crime prevention management'. For example, caretakers identified a large number of places in schools which burglars had used more than once to gain entry. These entry points might be better secured. Fire regulations seem to come into conflict with security at some schools, and better coordination between fire safety and security planning might lead to improvements in security. Schools might also look to the crime prevention implications of their day-to-day practices (for instance, in the use of audio-electronic equipment). None of these measures are particularly innovative or on an especially large scale but they may achieve reductions in burglary at relatively little cost. It is therefore suggested that local education authorities, with the help and advice of local police forces should look to small scale environmental and management improvements to reduce school burglary. These are most likely to be effective if they are applied selectively, concentrating effort in schools where burglary is most prevalent.

Broader implications
This study examined the variation of crime rates across a number of different school buildings. As such it used a 'cross-institutional' research design which, by using correlational methods of statistical analysis, can allow the contribution of individual factors affecting crime rates to be identified. This method has been frequently employed in the Home Office Research and Planning Unit's work both to evaluate processes of penal treatment (Clarke and Cornish, 1983) and, more recently, the role of situational factors in crime (Clarke and Mayhew, 1980). The method, however, is dependent upon the extent and nature of variation in crime rates and other variables in the sample under investigation. In this particular sample, the form of variation between schools has two important implications for the application of the situational approach to reducing school burglary.

In the first place, the individual design features of school buildings which contributed to their vulnerability (e.g. high perimeters, sprawling sites) were highly inter-related. In other words, they were all related aspects of school architecture. This is because the modern history of school building in Britain has been characterised by great waves of construction where many buildings were erected over a relatively short period, usually with standard building materials and techniques (Seaborne and Lowe, 1977). Consequently, exceptions to the general styles of building are relatively rare. This does, however, make it difficult to assess the effect of individual design features which might be modified in the interests of prevention. For example, it would have been difficult, using this sort of research design, to assess whether higher perimeter fences might reduce the risk of burglary at LMS schools since there were not enough examples of LMS schools with high perimeters to make a reliable statistical comparison with other LMS schools. This problem does impose a certain limitation on the usefulness of this study. In the absence of enough current exceptions to assess future piecemeal design modifications, we are faced with the prospect of either completely re-designing schools to remove everything associated with the LMS design tendency (which is unrealistic) or of experimenting rather blindly with piecemeal changes (which is rather risky and inefficient). It must be hoped that enough experience is eventually acquired so that more precise estimates of the effectiveness of individual design modifications can be made.

A second issue arising from the form of variation is the correlation between design features and social and organisational characteristics. SOC schools seem to possess a constellation of 'protective factors'. Chief among them is building design which provides fewer opportunities for burglary, but other factors may also be important – in particular, the beneficial ethos of small schools, their denominational character, and their lack of evening facilities which may render them unfamiliar to prospective burglars. It would seem that, as schools come more closely to resemble the LMS design tendency, the coalescence of protective factors begins to dissipate. As with the non-SOC schools in this sample, protection may be afforded by more variable or unique circumstances, which may account for the greater variation in burglary rates. Again, there needs to be a comparison between more non-SOC schools than in this sample if reliable conclusions are to be reached about the causes of this variation. Having established that SOC schools are fairly invulnerable to burglary, there seems no more need to consider them (and they are on the way out anyway). Rather, attention should be turned to finding out why some LMS schools have lower burglary rates than might be expected on the basis of their general design.

A final point is worth making about the likely motives of offenders. It appears there may be different objectives in school burglary – in particular, between nuisance burglars (presumably young adolescents) and serious professional or malicious burglars who may have more specific objectives such as theft or vandalism. However, this poses a problem for prevention. A prevention strategy which focused on providing greater security for school equipment (such as the use of safes, alarmed areas, etc.) might prevent professional burglary but might not affect nuisance burglary. A strategy which concentrated on making it difficult to break-into schools would probably affect all kinds of burglary but would be much more difficult to achieve (especially in the most vulnerable LMS schools). In this sense, preventing burglary in schools becomes a matter of choice between costs and benefits.

7 Preventing disorder

Malcolm Ramsay

Situational crime prevention has provided the focus, from one angle or another, for a rapidly increasing group of studies. An early project which sought to provide a broadly-based survey of the actual scope for situational measures is presented here (for a fuller report see Ramsay, 1982). In addition, some relevant developments both in research (Hope, 1985) and in policing (Hampshire Constabulary, 1985) are mentioned.

This study of the potential applicability of situational crime prevention was carried out by the Research and Planning Unit of the Home Office in 1981–2. By then, research had already shown that there was scope for a variety of individual measures aimed at 'designing out crime' (Clarke and Mayhew, 1980). In addition, Barry Poyner had assessed the preventability of street attacks or 'muggings' carried out in the open in central Birmingham and Coventry (Poyner, 1981 and 1983). Such studies provided the foundation for a further, more general investigation of the physical and social settings of criminal events. To what extent was it possible to analyse, to plot and to classify a wide range of crimes, in a way which would make sense for crime prevention purposes? Would such an audit suggest that sets of crimes occurred in circumstances which were sometimes sufficiently similar to facilitate the implementation of co-ordinated countermeasures, whereby crime might be reduced?

Pilot work carried out in the central parts of both a northern and a southern city suggested that crimes and other incidents dealt with by the police tended to be concentrated in particular locations or specific types of setting, and that they occurred more frequently at some periods of the day or week than at others (Ramsay and Heal, 1982). Interestingly, in each of the two cities, one of the more frequently occurring troublespots – this came as something of a surprise to both researchers and local police – was a hospital, beset by a considerable range and number of offences: the fact that such an unexpected setting for crime only showed up as a result of systematic analysis emphasised the potential value of the whole approach. It was evident that, in general, crime was less widespread in the suburban parts of the two cities than in their city-centre areas. This was in line with other research. For instance, Baldwin and Bottoms (1976), in their study of Sheffield, had noted that crimes decreased roughly in proportion to the distance from the centre of the city: they had emphasised the need to distinguish between the location of offences and the places of residence of offenders, whose home terrain may afford few appropriate targets or opportunities for crime.

The area chosen for the main study was central Southampton. By a narrow margin, Southampton ranks among the 20 largest cities in England and Wales: it is an important commercial centre and port, attracting many visitors and commuters, including, for instance, sailors and lorry drivers. The various outsiders who visit or work in Southampton use, together with local inhabitants, the wide range of leisure facilities in the city centre – clubs, pubs, restaurants, football ground, discos and other venues, together with the different forms of public transport – all of which, so the pilot work suggested, may be the setting for offences.

Within the geographical boundaries of the police sub-division for central Southampton – which is clearly defined on three out of four sides by the waterfront – as wide a range of crimes as possible was selected for analysis, making full use of the available police files. The reason for using these records – as opposed, say, to a victim survey, was that only a minority of those who were involved, in whatever capacity, in offences in the city centre area actually lived there. The remainder came either from the suburbs or from still further afield.

As it was, even the scrutiny of police records had to be limited in certain ways. Three substantial sets of offences – burglary, shoplifting and autocrime – were not studied. This was partly because they were each so distinct, partly because they have been the subject of a number of other studies in, admittedly, geographically different settings, and partly because there was often a lack of detailed information about them in police records (due to some extent to the fact that all three sorts of offence typically occurred surreptitiously). This still left for analysis a long list of essentially confrontational crimes of violence or disruption which, for various reasons, it was important to examine. First, there had not been many broadly-framed studies of crimes of violence since that by McClintock (1963). Second, offences of this kind were and are of particular concern to the public, both because of the threat they represent and also because of their prominent location. As a witness to one such incident in central Southampton commented, "I was horrified at seeing this sort of violence in the middle of a main street". Third, the pilot work had indicated that certain patterns were apparent in the timing, geographical distribution and circumstances of the many different kinds of crimes of violence or disruption committed in city-centre areas.

The records selected for examination were those dealing with crimes which occurred in central Southampton in the course of 1980: most of them related to offences which took place in the open or in places to which the public had access, although a small number involved disputes in private houses. The actual list comprised woundings of all degrees of seriousness, robbery, theft from the person, criminal damage (over £20), rape and indecent assault, together with a handful of rarer crimes: a murder (a 'domestic' incident), coupled with isolated cases of blackmail, child stealing, administering poison, and an affray. In addition, other sorts of offence of a rather less grave nature were examined, since they too involved public disruption if not violence: contraventions of the Public Order Act 1936, unlawful possession of an offensive weapon, criminal damage (under £20), obscene language, assault on a constable when resisting arrest, indecent exposure, obstruction of the highway, breach of the peace and, finally, a false telephone call. A further 118 such cases were traced and added to the 439 more serious ones, making a total of 557 instances of recorded crime which were incorporated in the survey.

The hallowed legal categories with which offenders are charged, some narrow and others extremely broad, have the effect, at times, of lumping together offences of an essentially different character, while on other occasions separating comparatively similar ones. This reflects the fact that they were originally formulated for the convenience of the courts, in days gone by, rather than with a view to facilitating crime prevention now. The legal terms were therefore discarded for the purposes of analysis in favour of a classification scheme derived from Poyner (1981 and 1983) which was designed to reflect the origins – and the settings – of the incidents, rather than the end result of the processing and labelling by police and courts. Six basic groups were identified, which were in turn subdivided in terms of locations, participants and sequences of events. These six main groups comprised violent disturbances (156), non-violent disturbances (35), clashes with police or security staff (53), sexual attacks or indecent behaviour (35), attacks or seizures for gain (46) and destruction of property (232). The first and last of these six categories – violent disturbances and destruction of property – together accounted for seven out of ten incidents.

Detailed examination indicated that, far from any of the six types of offence being random or liable to occur at any time or place, there were in fact distinct elements of patterning. In the first place, as other studies have found, the various crimes tended to occur in clusters at particular hours of the day, and days of the week. Over half the 557 incidents took place in the eight hour period starting at 22.00 or, in police terms, during the night shift. During the course of the week, almost half happened in the 48 hour period between 06.00 on Friday and the same time on Sunday morning. The 06.00 cut-off was chosen not only because it was the time when shifts changed over but also because, in social terms, midnight is not a satisfactory hour at which to divide one day from another (Poyner, 1981 and 1983). For anyone having a night out – and crime in central Southampton was more a matter of 'play' than of 'work' – the night need not end until long past midnight. In particular, incidents falling within the two largest categories, violent disturbances and destruction of property, tended to happen late at night, and towards the end of the week. This bunching of crimes at particular times of the day or week was placing a very uneven workload on the police. The recurrent need to respond to so large a proportion of all offences on Friday and Saturday nights was virtually taken for granted by police officers in central Southampton, despite the strain which this placed on them. Even a small reduction in trouble at these times would have been of great benefit to the police as well as to the public.

In ascertaining the scope for situational crime prevention, the key factor – even more important than the question of timing – is the extent to which crimes take place in the same or similar settings, and of course the extent to which these environments can be changed so as to become less criminogenic. Many of the offences which occurred in central Southampton in 1980 did indeed happen in contexts which offered some scope for constructive intervention. This can clearly be seen from Table 7.1.

Table 7.1 Settings of incidents in central Southampton (1980)

Setting	Number	Per cent
In or by pub/club	119	21.4
In or by other establishment	258	46.3
In street/park/open place	135	24.2
Domestic setting	45	8.1
Total	557	100.0

More than two-thirds of the 557 crimes were situated in or by pubs, clubs or other places open to the public, rather than just anywhere in the open.

Indeed, over half the 119 offences which took place in or by pubs and clubs involved a mere dozen premises. One establishment was implicated in 11 crimes, while a group of clubs close to each other (in St Mary's Street) was involved in a total of 29 cases, the various High Street pubs in 11, and a further four clubs in three or four cases each. In terms both of disorder and of demands on the police, these offences represented something of the tip of an iceberg: there were additional incidents at these locations, to some of which the police were summoned, which did not result in any crime being recorded, even though there may have been some sort of trouble. Quite a few offences took place at closing time – at 02.00 typically, in the case of clubs with late licences – when there was apt to be violence and vandalism near to these places. Attempts to police the departure of high spirited clients did not always prove successful. Occasionally they may even have been counter-productive.

Was this kind of disorder inevitable? It would certainly be unrealistic to think of eliminating it altogether. However, the fact is that some pubs and clubs, not very different from those notable for their disorder, managed to avoid repeated incidents. In the case of one such club, previously well-run, which started to give cause for concern in the course of the year selected for the research (1980), the police contacted the management committee: thereafter, as the club tightened up (for instance on entrance requirements), and as this became known, a greater orderliness prevailed. Close liaison of this kind between police and management was however the exception rather than the rule at the time of the research.

The responsibility for ensuring that pubs and clubs (and other places of entertainment) operate in a relatively trouble-free manner necessarily rests, in large part, with those who own or manage them: it is neither realistic nor desirable for the police to have to visit them with any frequency and, obviously, they are at least

84

internally, out of sight from street patrols. Where establishments fail to live up to their responsibilities, they may then need to be persuaded to do so by police or magistrates, perhaps with the aid of a certain degree of pressure, but certainly on the basis of detailed information.

The way in which managers or owners can best minimise the likelihood of disorder is by paying close attention to the promotion of a proper, orderly ambience, in which patrons are likely to relax and feel secure (Engstad and Evans, 1980). Quarrels and fights are typically the result of overcrowded or inadequately organised settings. For instance – in Southampton – a regular Saturday night visitor to one of the clubs went instead on a Sunday night, without realising, due to the lack of any warning, that this was homosexuals' night: he was propositioned, and violence then ensued. In such situations, having bouncers may be part of the answer but, especially given the difficulty of finding suitably tactful as well as hefty staff, it is unlikely to solve matters altogether. Factors which are at least equally important in ensuring that establishments run smoothly include permitted numbers of patrons, membership rules, decor, lighting, entertainment, the provision of food, times of opening and the manner in which 'closing time' is carried through.

The importance of tackling violence in licensed premises is underlined by the fact that 56 of the 156 violent crimes which took place in central Southampton in 1980 occurred in or by pubs and clubs. Obviously, for the owners or managers, there is a need to consider the cost of any efforts to prevent disorder – though disorder itself may not enhance profitability. Striking an appropriate balance is never going to be easy. In that the full costs of repeated incidents – the costs of injuries, of damage to nearby property, of policing and of other after-the-event legal action – need to be taken into account not just by the wider community but also by those running places where these incidents have originated; the police, where necessary, have a role to play in enlightening managers as to the consequences of a badly run establishment.

The 258 offences which happened in or by establishments other than pubs and clubs involved so great a variety of settings that it is rather more difficult to specify precise ways in which those managing them might minimise the possibility of disorder. Among the many places involved were shops, restaurants, the hospital, the football ground, the various different transport undertakings and welfare agencies. In a few cases, one complicating factor was an inter-racial dimension, which exacerbated certain incidents in restaurants and take-aways open late at night. While it can indeed be difficult for these places to control boisterous customers, especially if racial hostility is unleashed, some establishments seem to be better able than others to handle awkward customers satisfactorily. The police have a part to play in helping to awaken managers to the need to review the circumstances in which disorder arises just as much as in responding to incidents when they actually occur: the provision of advice should be seen as no more than a logical counterpart to the dispatch of emergency response patrols. The same general principles apply as in the case of pubs and clubs in that, essentially, it is for the management of any place open to the public to ensure that the scope for disorder is minimised. For instance, welfare agencies which keep clients waiting for hours on end should not find it altogether surprising if mounting frustrations occasionally lead to trouble: a need to review arrangements for queuing and appointments is evident. Or, to give another example, in public toilets, any lack of secure locks and inviolable partitions is apt to lead to incidents.

Not all the 258 incidents in or by establishments other than pubs and clubs lent themselves equally well to the adoption of preventive measures by their managements. The 'unfocused' acts of damage to shops, offices and commercial premises were particularly problematic (these were cases where, typically, damage occurred late in the evening, in the general vicinity of, or on routes away from places of entertainment). In that the targets commonly singled out were large, plate-glass windows costing, in 1980, up to £1,000 or more, one way of reducing at least the cost of this kind of destruction would be to use smaller panes of glass. Such a policy, however, not only implies alterations which would themselves be costly, but also conflicts with the need to attract customers as powerfully as possible: a classic conflict of interest of the kind which not infrequently bedevils crime prevention (Hope and Murphy, 1983; Hope, 1985). However, the majority of the 258 offences involving places open to the public were not of this kind, but had their roots in circumstances which, at least in theory, were susceptible to control by management.

Ultimately, the limiting factor was that, in comparison with pubs and clubs, the offences associated with other public establishments were widely dispersed. The 258 offences at or by these places involved no less than 160 different locations. The football ground with nine offences and the local hospital with eight were by far the largest concentrations. Looking at the general run of offences, while it could be said, at least with hindsight, that some places apparently operated in a way that was conducive to trouble, actual crimes typically only resulted perhaps two or three times a year at the one and same place. The effort involved in seeking to eliminate such offences should not be underestimated. Conflicting priorities were already in evidence. For instance, one of the two robberies of shops (the only serious one), which took place in a busy department store, probably only succeeded because a security lock which was meant to impede access to the cash office had been dispensed with, business being unusually busy at the time. Crimes of violence and disorder are rare events: remote eventualities quite possibly cushioned by insurance. This is not to say that nothing more can be done, but that, for the most part, it will not be easy to do better. In this way, a certain amount of crime is almost built into the modern city-centre area.

Apart from the small group of offences which happended in domestic settings (to which it is hard to envisage any systematic countermeasure), the one remaining group of crimes consists of those which occurred in the open. Typically, these were events which happened either in the street or in a park, and which did not have an identifiable link with any specific pub, club or other establishment. On the one hand, these offences, occurring as they did in the open, presented problems for intervention since, apart from increasing very substantially (at prohibitive expense) the number of relevant police patrols, their circumstances or settings could not be altered very readily. On the other hand, precisely because they occurred outside the usual context of crime – such as licensed premises late at night – they represented a specially important problem, and one worth probing further. Altogether, there were 135 such offences, of which no less than 82 involved either attacks for gain or sexual attacks or some other form of interpersonal violence. The victims of these 82 incidents generally had no prior knowledge of the person or people who attacked them, a point which underlines the seriousness of this particular set of incidents.

Although these 135 offences occurred in the open, this did not mean that they took place absolutely at random. It is true that in terms of their timing they were distributed comparatively evenly throughout the day and the week (compounding the difficulty of mounting successful police patrols to counter them). In geographical terms at least, there was some comparatively marked clustering of incidents. One such group of, in all, 12 offences, including two of the four relatively serious sexual attacks on women, took place in the various parks and open spaces in central Southampton. A second group, altogether more numerous (29) if less serious individually, occurred in two continuous, partly pedestrianised streets (Above Bar, Bargate). In both cases environmental intervention would be a possibility. The parks, which are currently quite open, could be fenced in, which would reduce their attractiveness to daytime assailants worried about making good their escape and would also make it possible to have the parks closed altogether at night. As for the two continuous streets, strategically placed television cameras, relayed to the local police station, might reduce lawlessness to some extent. In each of these cases, however, likely gains would probably be small in relation to the cost and inconvenience and infringement of personal liberty incurred. After all, even in the case of the two continuous streets one is talking about little more than an offence a fortnight, and not necessarily a particularly serious one at that. And were these drastic measures nonetheless adopted at both locations, it is probable that any reduction in crime there would merely be a small one, since the various countermeasures would only be likely to have a limited effect.

The very scarcity of crime, then, restricts the development and application of situational crime prevention. The overall total of 557 crimes of violence and disorder recorded by the police in central Southampton amounts, on average, to less than two per day – a good many of which were fairly trivial. Given that crime is in fact comparatively rare, at least to judge by this study of a single city centre, it is significant that the situational approach is still relevant. In particular, certain pubs and clubs offer a measure of scope for this kind of tactic, as to a lesser extent, do various other establishments. What this study has certainly shown is that, far from occurring at random, crimes tend to be linked either directly or indirectly to particular settings – which is precisely the basic presupposition underlying the situational approach to crime prevention.

Similar research to the Southampton project has been undertaken more recently by Hope, who has come up with comparable findings (Hope, 1985). Hope's study, which has as its setting central Newcastle, incorporates a lengthy analysis of obstacles to the implementation of measures aimed at preventing crime. The design of the empirical aspect of his research differs somewhat from that used for Southampton: Hope's data were extracted from police occurrence sheets – which are used to log all incidents to which the police are summoned, regardless of their nature – not simply from files for recorded crimes. Furthermore, Hope only concerned himself with Friday and Saturday nights – the paramount importarce of these two periods (06.00 to 18.00) being evident from the work of Poyner (1981 and 1983) as well as the Southampton study.

In central Newcastle as in Southampton, certain pubs and clubs were prominent sources of disorder, particularly around closing time (15 per cent of public houses accounted for 42 per cent of all disorder associated with licensed premises, while around a quarter of all such disorderly incidents took place in the half hour between 22.30 and 23.00). Hope analyses the social organisation and control of drinking, both of which he describes as being – in their own ways – highly fragmented. He emphasises the need not simply for piecemeal action to modify the more troublesome kind of setting in which drinking takes place but also for regular close liaison between major breweries (who own many city-centre public houses, which they operate through managers appointed by them), the police, local authorities and Licensing Justices, all of whom need to work together to have the greatest possible impact on the disorder which stems from problematic public houses and other licensed premises. As Hope points out, such co-operation is never going to be easy to achieve or to sustain but is, nevertheless, essential.

In just the last few years, police forces throughout England and Wales have shown increasing interest in the systematic mapping and analysis of incidents at the local level – for targeting police manpower and for preventing crime with greater effectiveness. It would not be practicable to provide an overall survey here. However, it would scarcely be appropriate to conclude this chapter without some mention of recent developments in Southampton itself (Hampshire Constabulary, 1985). The plotting and listing of crimes has been carried out with care, and with successive improvements. This has made it possible to reorganise foot beats and to allocate patrols to those areas most in need of attention, with enhanced precision – and also, on occasion, to explain to members of the public why such changes are necessary, by way of reassurance. Problems of measurement have, as usual, made it difficult overall to quantify the measure of 'success' which local police management reckon to have achieved. However, an apparent reduction in the number of violent incidents not only had a beneficial impact by lessening fear of crime on the part of some members of the public, but also caused police officers themselves to feel less apprehensive about weekend violence.

One important achievement on the part of the police in Southampton was to tackle the continuing spate of incidents associated with three particular clubs. In the case of one of these strongly-worded advice was given, while in the case of the two others the problems were of such magnitude that – on the basis of all the carefully gathered information – the renewal of their licences was opposed. So marked was the contrast between maps showing patterns of street-crime before and after closure, due to the reduced number of assaults, thefts of and from motor vehicles, thefts of cycles and criminal damage, in the area around the two clubs that, when these maps were subsequently produced in court to sustain the witholding of the licences, they had a 'considerable impact' (Hampshire Constabulary, 1985).

On the basis of the Southampton research, itself buttressed by other findings such as those from Newcastle, it is evident that situational crime prevention has a firm foundation in reality. Much violence and disorder occurs in well-defined sorts of settings – settings which it should be possible to modify effectively, although perhaps only with considerable difficulty. Leaving aside all the problems of implementation, the other drawback to situational crime prevention is that, while it is undoubtedly relevant to a large number of offences, the extent to which absolutely identical settings are involved time after time is rather limited – doubtless in part because crime itself is a comparatively rare phenomenon. In the cse of central Southampton, a handful of pubs and clubs, a hospital and one or two other spots were the only individual places which gave rise to a succession of crimes of violence and disorder. Nevertheless, if situational crime prevention has its drawbacks, it would be as well to emphasise that other more conventional methods for dealing with crime have their own limitations (Clarke and Hough, 1984). Increasingly, it is now being recognised that the notion – in vogue for some two hundred years – that there must be a simple answer to crime (if only it can be discovered/applied) is, quite simply, one that is illusory. Situational crime prevention takes its proper place alongside the various older strategies, both it and they being merely partial solutions to an intractable problem.

8 Neighbourhood crime control and the police: a view of the American experience

George Kelling

The failure of the American criminal justice system to protect citizens from the depredation of disorder and crime has given rise to a powerful grass-roots movement: community crime control. Although the broadest definition of community crime control encompasses a wide variety of individual and collective self-protective activities (e.g. Guardian Angels who patrol subways and neighbourhoods, and the creation of arbitration panels). The focus of this paper will be the collective actions of citizens in neighbourhood organizations.

This paper makes two assumptions:

community crime control activities reduce crime and fear; and,

community crime control activities are legitimate collective activities by citizens to protect themselves and their property and warrant sustained support by police.

The first assumption arises out of the author's personal experiences and beliefs, and is supported by a recently published synthesis of the community crime control literature by Greenberg, Rohe and Williams (1984). The synthesis concludes, among other things, that there is a general consensus in the literature that collective neighbourhood efforts can influence crime and fear of crime (see also Titus, 1982). This consensus is shared by most participants in community crime control groups.

As is apparent, the first assumption is utilitarian: community crime control works. The second assumption is a statement of professional and political values. It asserts that legitimate bases of social control exist intermediate to the polarities of self-induced individual restraint and the legal coercive authority of the state. These sources of control include family (nuclear and extended), church, industry, and bureaucratic, professional and political organizations, as well as neighbourhoods and communities. All can be supported or impeded in their attempts to reduce crime and fear by police actions.

This paper begins with a detailed discussion of community crime control in a large northeastern city in the United States and then discusses three issues: (1) the difference between the research presented here and that presented in the community crime control literature which tends to concentrate on groups that have been sponsored and/or initiated by governmental or philanthropic organizations; (2) the bases of the success of the community crime control movement and the potentials for disagreement between groups and police; and, (3) the dangers which inhere in the community crime control movement.

Community crime control in Northeastern City

Collective activities by citizens to protect themselves and their communities from crime are rooted in the ancient Anglo-Saxon custom of social obligation: each citizen is required to come to the aid of others in distress or to pursue villains who commit crimes. So strong was this custom in early England that workers were obliged to keep weapons handy to enable them to pursue and subdue offenders. Beyond these English legal roots, however, collective activities by citizens in America exist within the context of a rich and controversial political tradition which asserts that participation in self-governing community activities profoundly shapes individual character, as well as social and political life. Both historical traditions and their peculiar American expression must be kept in mind when reviewing community crime control in America.

There are over 100 identifiable community crime control groups in Northeastern City. All have names, meet with relative regularity, and either have been, or are now, involved in some form of anti-crime work (e.g. block watch, escort service, or neighbourhood patrol). Few groups, probably no more than three or four, have received external financial support. The modest funds which some groups have come from small-scale fund-raising activities such as street fairs, bake sales, or occasional levees against members. Generally, whatever funds are raised offset the costs of a local newsletter or purchase of equipment. Equipment is modest: although some groups have gone through fairly substantial fund-raising activities to purchase equipment such as walky-talkies for patrol, they are for the most part, unused. The most often purchased form of equipment is whistles. Usually these whistles are given to members and non-members of the groups alike (often in a friendly attempt to recruit additional members).

For the most part, groups thrive in relatively small neighbourhood areas – one, two, or three faceblocks; one to four square blocks; several faceblocks leading to a "T" intersection plus one block each way on the T etc. The organizations usually represent about 50 households each, although a few are considerably larger – up to 500 members. Most groups claim that their total composition is demographically representative of their neighbourhoods, however, the impression one gets from meetings is that one racial group tends to be most active and thus dominate the active membership. For the most part, groups strive to be representative of their neighbourhoods, occasionally including street-users as well as residents: one group has attempted to include in their anti-crime activities a "bag-lady" (a homeless woman who, for the most part, lives on the street) who stays in their neighbourhood. Invited by residents, she attended a special neighbourhood meeting on rape. Although silent during most of the meeting, she surprised the group with an account of being raped. Since then, members pay special attention to her during patrol.

A few groups give the impression of wanting to protect their neighbourhoods from incursions by strangers (e.g. racial minorities), although members are quite delicate and sophisticated in their expression of these tendencies. Such groups are exceptions, however. Members of many groups testify to the broadening nature of their anti-crime activities: contacts and activities with persons of other races or sexual inclinations have taught members how desirous of order and community harmony almost all citizens are. Such values aside, members have come to learn that racist policies are unproductive – groups either work together or remain divided and vulnerable to predators or persons who would capitalize on community divisions.

Most groups meet fortnightly or monthly. Attendance at meetings is low, generally somewhere between 6 to 15 people, relative to the total membership of the group. Meetings are generally announced via distributed fliers and held in members' homes (occasionally in a church or community agency) on a weekday during the evening. Coffee, soft drinks and sweets are generally served – wine or beer are served at a few. As members arrive, idle neighbourhood conversation ensues (who's had a baby, who's ill or has died, what else is going on in the community, etc.). Business meetings generally follow and are relatively brief. Most often, meetings begin with reports about crime and disorder based on informal neighbourhood information occasionally supplemented by official crime statistics furnished in advance by the police or brought to meetings by a police official. Reports on other issues and the development of community responses (patrols, watches, etc.) follow. Meetings generally close with socializing.

Most such groups have been in existence for several years – many for 5 to 10 years, and at least one for 25 years. Generally, they originated in one of two ways: they "spun-off" a larger local voluntary organization through the activities of several neighbours; or through the independent local organizing activities of several neighbours. In either case, most groups were organized after a dramatic criminal event or in response to a chronic neighbourhood problem such as street walkers or drug dealers. Although most groups identify themselves as concentrating exclusively on crime, discussion reveals that many groups define anti-crime activities broadly. One such group, for example, identified getting city officials to provide it with trees to plant as its most successful anti-crime activity.

Leadership in community anti-crime groups is informal but stable: generally those who initially organize groups assume leadership and their leadership persists over a considerable period of time. Leadership is shared or transferred most often when the leader(s) wants relief from responsibility. Cabals are rare. Responsibility for minutes (which probably exist in less than 50% of the groups), notifications for meetings, handouts and fliers, and other paperwork, generally is shared by people who have access to copiers and other equipment, and by other persons who have the time during the day to either draft or distribute materials. Likewise, if technical skills are needed (legal, for example), they are provided by persons in the group.

On occasion, government officials attend meetings. Most often, the official is a member of the community relations office of the police department and relations between the officer and groups are cordial: the officer is almost always genuinely sympathetic to the goals and methods of the group and eager to provide whatever assistance in the form of information or consultation s/he can. That the officer is limited to the provision of information and consultation is simply assumed. Rarely does a local patrol officer attend meetings. Groups know the name of their pre-cinct commanders and are likely to have met with them in the not-too-distant past.

Meetings with other governmental officials generally take place in those officials' offices, although most contacts are by telephone. These contacts deal with light-ing, snow-plowing, trees (getting them planted), street maintenance, garbage col-lection, and other services. The agency about which citizens' groups are most con-cerned, however, is the police department. On rare occasions, groups might have some contact with the prosecutor's office; they practically never meet with judges or correctional officials.

During years in which local political elections are held, community groups provide forums between political candidates and citizens. Generally, meetings between political figures and community groups are given considerable publicity and are held in more public locations: churches, agencies, etc. Although few groups pub-licly endorse candidates, recent elections in several cities have alerted groups to the potential of neighbourhood political activity: mayors and other city officials have been elected who have run on platforms which strongly endorsed the impor-tance of neighbourhood oversight in urban governance, including police.

Although many groups developed out of somewhat larger voluntary associations, they maintain relatively little ongoing contact with those or other crime control groups. They are aware of other groups, know them by name, know some of the participants, but co-ordination of routine anti-crime activities such as patrol is rare. In emergencies, such as a missing child, groups rally together quickly and can maintain high levels of co-ordinated activities for days. Moreover, some have learned to co-ordinate their activities when approaching governmental agencies or political officers.

This latter co-ordination is the result of a perception which has developed in many groups that such agencies tend to play anti-crime groups off against each other. For example, a member of a relatively small but politically active neighbourhood group explained to the author while patrolling together one evening that over the past several years neighbourhood groups had learned to work together when approaching "city hall". Noting the ethnic and racial composition of his commun-ity – his neighbourhood was, for the most part white: adjacent neighbourhoods were largely Spanish-speaking or black – he explained that whenever any of the groups planned to approach city hall about some major issue, they would routinely "line up sights" among themselves before taking action. They have learned in the past that an often heard response to requests was, "Well, if we do this for you, we'd have to the same for X or Y group". Groups endorsed by, or collaborating with, competitors neutralize attempts to play one off against another.

Additionally, a city-wide network of neighbourhood crime control organizations has developed under the leadership of a local private non-profit making criminal justice agency. Operating with funds provided by local businesses and philanthropies, as well as a large nationally known foundation, this network meets both monthly, and on an *ad hoc* emergency basis. Monthly meetings deal with issues of crime and disorder which result from city-wide policies or practices but which affect neighbourhood groups. A major revision of police tactics or changes in prosecutorial policies about the handling of drug dealers are examples of such issues. *Ad hoc* meetings are usually held in response to some city-wide emergency or problem. Any statements which emerge from these meetings are carefully drafted to ensure that no neighbourhood group believes its autonomy or interests are threatened. Despite such successful collaborative efforts, however, groups guard their independence – some fiercely.

Most groups' anti-crime activities consist of patrol and neighbourhood watches, neighbourhood watches being the more prevalent. Groups that patrol generally do so according to some pattern: some on weekends; others, during particular hours (early evening, for example, when people are returning from work); others, during the summer when prostitutes and drug dealers are especially active on streets; yet others, during the winter when neighbours are returning from school or work and days are short. Patrol practices depend on the members' periodic diagnoses of the problems confronting their community. Some groups patrol for a time and then, when the problem is alleviated, slacken off – picking up when members perceive that problems are on the upswing. Members worry somewhat during slack times that membership will not become active again in the future, but most seem to have come to accept this periodicity of activities.

Residents generally patrol in groups of two or more although one person patrolling alone is not unusual. When patrolling residential areas, residents usually greet all citizens in polite terms. Neighbours are greeted by name, followed by some brief conversation. Strangers are greeted courteously with some identification of the patrollers as members of a neighbourhood group – the assumption being that all citizens, including strangers, will be comforted by the presence of vigilant citizens. (That citizens who may be inclined to wrongdoing will not feel this way is a source of wry humour for those who patrol – believing that as long as patrollers are polite, strangers have no basis to object to civil enquiries or greetings.) Patrollers are instructed not to carry weapons. If some difficulty arises, their general operating principles are to make noise and call for official help. Intervention in a criminal event other than by creation of a commotion is advocated only if someone's physical safety is threatened. The obligation of neighbours not patrolling is to respond to any hue and cry by calling police, turning on lights, and/or coming outdoors.

Rarely, but with increasing frequency, groups are beginning to rely on demonstrations and publicity to deal with serious chronic problems – especially street prostitution and drug dealing. As a rule, they resort to such tactics only after they have come to believe that they cannot get adequate protection and assistance from police and other criminal justice agencies. Participation in such militant activities

95

cuts across social class. In a poor minority area, drug dealers have become so out-rageous that citizens have taken to the streets and publicly demonstrated for more police and governmental action against them. In a gentrified area adjacent to hotels and restaurants, citizens have resorted to similar actions for dealing with street prostitution. Members of the neighbourhood group regularly get out on the streets with prostitutes and, by their presence, attempt to intimidate both prosti-tutes and their clients. Additionally, members of the group, including lawyers and other professionals, have successfully pushed for legislative, political, and organi-zational action. One successful activity led to restrictions on the type of part-time work in which police officers can be involved. Believing that officers who were employed off-duty by bars sided with their employer barkeepers when disputes arose between them and citizens about noise and after hours activities, citizens successfully pushed for actions to restrict police officers from working part-time in bars.

In sum, the vast majority of community crime control groups are small neighbour-hood groups that operate with modest, if any, funds and no professional staff. Although a small percentage of members meet regularly, they are "caretakers" of neighbourhood interests. They meet regularly to catch up on neighbourhood gos-sip, discuss problems in the area, and plan activities. The larger membership con-venes around block parties and occasional emergencies. (Often non-members participate in these activities as well as members.) Specific crime-control activities are practiced inconsistently – occasionally because of lack of group vitality, but more often because of a group's perception of need. For the most part, groups are self-contained: they organize themselves, manage their own affairs, mobilize themselves in emergencies, and jealously guard their autonomy.

Research in Northeastern City and the literature
This portrayal of the community crime control movement departs from that which dominates the literature. The emphasis in the literature is on external organizing, charismatic leadership, ongoing funding, professional staff, and professionalized formal structure. (Yin 1982; Mayer and Blake 1980; Greenberg et al., 1984; Warren and Warren 1977; Ross 1979; Rich, 1980.) Although there are groups in Northeastern City that fit this characterization, they are in a vast minority, repre-senting less than five per cent of the total number of groups.

Several factors may account for the difference between groups described in the crime control literature and those in Northeastern City: the characteristics of Northeastern City; the bias inherent when funders write about projects they fund or for which they commission evaluations; or, the bias inherent when practicing organizers (whether community or organization based) write prescriptively about their approaches or projects. Arguably, the latter two explanation are more plaus-ible than the first, although it must be conceded that Northeastern City is not a typical American city – it is an old city comprised of many ethnic neighbourhoods. Nevertheless, there is evidence that such grass roots organizations are flourishing throughout the country. New York City is known to have 15,000 block associa-

96

tions, with 30 per cent of them reporting that crime prevention is their single most important activity (Citizens Report, 1984). Yin (1982) notes a previously unreported finding:

> ...there appear to be numerous patrols across the country, in neighbourhoods of varied income and racial composition...Most of the patrols, other than those organized by public housing authorities, receive no public financial support.

Crenson (1984) has described the working of comparable grass roots organizations in Baltimore. Moreover, conversations with citizens and officials in other cities suggest that the pattern of anti-crime groups in Northeastern City is far from atypical: grass roots organizations are developing rapidly throughout cities in the United States. This point is not a mere academic nicety. If, as is suggested, community crime control groups are primarily grass roots organizations without need of funds or staff, they are neither children of, nor dependent on, criminal justice, governmental, or other professional or quasi-professional organizations. And, as will be discussed below, although community crime control groups are not political *organizations,* they are part of a political movement: their activities heighten members' social and political sensitivities.

Neighbourhood groups and police

Greenberg and colleagues (1984) conclude that three activities of community crime control groups explain their impact. The first two are the direct result of citizens' actions on their own behalf:

> (i) increased informal interaction among citizens; and
>
> (ii) active patrol, crime watch, escort service and other anti-crime efforts.

The third is both direct and indirect – citizens' action on their own behalf and citizen action to capture other resources:

> improved physical surroundings (citizens take action on their own to improve their neighbourhoods and to capture other resources – trees from city government, for example, to improve their physical environment).

The literature on foot patrol suggests a fourth citizen route to the reduction of fear and crime, (Police Foundation, 1980; Trojanowicz, 1981):

> the ability of neighbourhood groups to capture particular forms of police service e.g. foot patrol, and more broadly, the ability of citizens to shape police, prosecutorial, judicial and correctional decision-making.

The latter two indirect efforts are of interest here – not because direct activities such as patrol are unimportant, but because most groups in Northeastern City are competent to manage direct activities with little or no assistance from governmental or philanthropic agencies. Indirect activities are different: they require organizational and political activities to acquire improved or increased governmental services: garbage collection and street repair, for example.

Most citizen activities to gain improved or increased services are routine and handled via telephone – agencies often welcome information about problems or needs, and take appropriate and timely action. On other occasions, citizens may have more ambitious long term goals – planting trees along a roadway, for example – that are congruent with the interests of agencies. In such circumstances a scenario not unlike the following is conceivable: community and agency representatives meet several times and *quid pro quo* results: the city provides the trees and citizens the labour. The delivery and planting of trees takes place with varying degrees of ceremony – it could include participation of high-level officials and press – thereby pleasing everyone. The neighbourhood gets trees, the city good relations and press.

When citizens push for scarce goods or services, however, the process becomes considerably more complicated. City departments may not have trees or, if they do, may not be willing to collaborate with citizens in distributing and planting them. In the case of police, they may not want to increase services in particular neighbourhood areas. Even more complicated are circumstances in which citizens want *different services*. And, in the United States at least, different services are often what citizens want from police. Greenberg and her colleagues (1984), for example, note the demand for different police services when discussing the results of a national conference on community crime control:

> one of the major themes that emerged...was that police are very important in community crime prevention, but in ways that have little to do with traditional policing. Activities that were stressed include controlling incivilities; providing complete, accurate, and ongoing information on the local crime problem to community crime groups, providing a sense among citizens that help is available when needed; enhancing trust of external institutions; and assisting in the mediation of intergroup conflicts.

Such demands put police in a quandary. They have inherited a carefully crafted organizational strategy, institutional capacity, and professional culture – all legacies of late 19th and early 20th century perceptions of how best to police cities and insulate police from what reformers saw as the corroding effects of close linkages to communities. Citizens, frustrated about the levels of disorder and crime, yet largely dependent on police for the success of their own efforts, have their own ideas and strategy for dealing with neighbourhood problems. As police and citizens attempt to "line up sights", the following positions frame the conduct of business:

> police see their role as crime control and solving crimes; citizens want police to improve the quality of urban life and create feelings of personal security;
>
> police want to structure impersonal relations with citizens and neighbourhoods; citizens want intimate relations with police;
>
> police want to be independent of political and neighbourhood control – they view political accountability as tantamount to corruption; citizens want police to be accountable to neighbourhoods – inevitably a form of political accountability;

police tactics emphasize automobile preventive patrol and rapid response to calls for service; citizens want foot patrol;

police see themselves as the "thin blue line" between order and chaos; citizens see themselves as the primary source of control backed up by police, and

police emphasize centralized efficiency; citizens desire decentralized operations and local decision-making.

And so, a "dance" begins between citizens and police. Rarely, however, do they understand that they are dancing to different tunes. Citizens demand police involvement in "community crime control". With enthusiasm and commitment varying greatly both within and between police departments, police initiate programs. Most often, the programs include operation identification, community relations, some organizing help, home security consultation, and information sharing. Police locate crime-prevention activities in crime control or community relations units and sequester officers for such activities. The officers are generally highly motivated and relations between citizens and crime prevention officers harmonious: officers appreciate, or come to appreciate, citizens' contributions to crime control; officers share citizens values; citizens recognize this and cordially receive officers' advice and assistance. (All of these characteristics separate crime-prevention officers from the dominant view of their organization and culture and place them, in the opinion of many of their peers, in the "empty holster crowd" – that is, as not being "real" cops.) Whether citizens know it or not at the outset of their contacts with crime-prevention officers, they quickly learn that crime prevention officers are outside of the mainstream of policing without power to make any decisions about policing in neighbourhoods.

In the rest of the police department, business proceeds as usual. Citizens rarely get to know officers who patrol their neighbourhoods: officers whisk in and out of neighbourhoods as rapidly as possible. Command staff personnel occasionally meet with groups, sometimes on their own initiative, at other times in response to requests from citizens. Police discuss serious crimes; citizens, disorder or minor crimes such as prostitution and low-level drug dealing. Predictably, citizens demand improved and different services; police commanders cite staff shortages, other priorities, and the shortcomings of the rest of the criminal justice system as bases for not being able to respond to citizens' requests or demands. If the command personnel are district or precinct commanders, their situation in most American police departments is often not all that different than crime prevention officers: since authority for tactical or personnel changes rests higher up the chain of command, they could not respond to most citizen requests even if they so desired. Often, the result of such meetings is continual wrangling and mutual frustration. On some occasions, especially in minority communities, hostility results with citizens believing that police are uncaring and police believing citizens are ungrateful.

On occasion, an unusually persistent citizens' group will succeed in modifying patrol practices in that group's neighbourhood, but only as the result of extensive and prolonged political activity. An example of such persistence is found in the neighbourhood (described earlier) adjacent to a hotel and restaurant area which was besieged by prostitution. Having developed political "clout", they wrenched regular foot patrols out of the department. For most neighbourhoods, however, such is not the case. As a consequence, one is struck by the limited influence of police in neighbourhoods. Police departments increase or decrease their size, reorganize, develop different tactics, or ostensibly modify their practices in a variety of other ways, yet such changes go largely unnoticed. Yates (1979), for example, notes the limited influence of government in other areas of urban service delivery as well:

> ...at the level of day-to-day problems, it is neighbourhood residents who turn stoops and cars into recreation areas, sidewalks and streets into playing fields, and unadorned playground basketball courts into neighbourhood institutions. Compared with this resourcefulness and adaptiveness, city efforts such as the "vest-pocket parks" seem artificial and lifeless...Thus there are street-level resources that are used every day to adapt to unpleasant conditions and to affect resident's lives in specific ways.

The above is sad; most research which sheds light on the relationship between police and citizens suggests their mutual dependence. Police need familiar relations with citizens for legitimacy to act, information to solve crimes, improved morale and job satisfaction, and their own personal safety. Citizens need close relations with police for back-up force to control streets, ensure their safety, provide emergency service and assistance in the prevention of crime, and to restrain them when their actions verge on vigilanteism. (Police Foundation 1981; Trojanowicz 1983; Trojanowicz and Banas, 1985a; Eck 1983; Wilson and Kelling 1982; Moore and Kelling 1983.)

As discouraging as some of the above discussion about the relationship between community anti-crime groups and police may appear, there are reasons to be more optimistic. Police, in the United States at least, are at a watershed. Research and their own experience has taught them that their potential to prevent or reduce crime is limited. Once relatively insulated from the vagaries of urban budgetting, police have faced the budgetcutters' axes in many cities. The myths that police can "do it alone" and that crime-fighting is professionals' business, that citizens should stay out of are largely dead. A new conventional wisdom that emphasizes order maintenance, fear reduction, the quality of urban life as a measure of success of police (rather than just crime levels), problem solving (rather than mere responding to incidents) (Goldstein 1979), closer working relations between police and citizens, neighbourhood beats, and use of foot patrols is gaining a substantial foothold in many urban police departments. These include New York, N.Y., Houston, Texas, Newark, N.J., Los Angeles, CA., Minneapolis, MN., Boston, MA., and many others (Moore and Kelling 1983).

The current problem is that implementation of these concepts lags behind their intellectual adoption. Although cities are committed to reorienting their police departments, the tradition of police tactics based on preventive patrol in automobiles and the burden of 911 systems (emergency rapid response to all calls for service) have complicated and delayed implementation of tactics based on the emerging new conventional wisdom of policing. At the heart of this wisdom is the idea that to solve community problems, police must work intimately with citizens to diagnose the nature of problems and devise solutions. Those solutions may involve police action, but they may not as well. Often the resolution of problems will be found in the action of citizens, neighbourhoods, private sector organizations, or other governmental organizations.

Finally, what many police executives in the United States – even those initially quite skeptical about community policing – seem to be learning, is that closer relations with citizens has strong potential for strengthening police organizations. It does so in the following ways:

first, its appeal to citizens is so strong that it elicits strong political and fiscal support from citizens. In Flint, Michigan, for example, citizens voted to increase their taxes (rates) to ensure the continuation of community foot patrols. This was during a period of drastic fiscal retrenchment in Flint;

second, close police relations with neighbourhoods seems to offer the only identifiable strategy through which police stand a reasonable chance of improving their capability of preventing, reducing, and solving crimes. True, it is an indirect means – police must work through citizens and other groups – yet in contrast with their current inability to improve their capabilities, prudent police administrators would seem to be well-advised to exploit the potential of working closely with communities (Pate *et al*, 1976; Skogan and Antunnes, 1979; Eck, 1983);

third, the popularity of police tactics which bring police and citizens into stronger collaborative relations has great potential for developing the kind of support for police required to maintain order in cities, especially during periods of urban unrest. The mobilization of the "good people" of a community in support of police is essential for the maintenance of urban order (Wilson and Kelling, 1982);

fourth, police morale is improved and the police occupation is enhanced by the activities associated with working closely with communities (Police Foundation, 1980; Trojanowicz, 1981), and

finally, there is evidence that police feel, and are, safer when working closely with citizens and citizen's groups (Trojanowicz and Banas, 1985b).

Dangers in the crime control movement
On the other hand, there are at least four dangers which inhere in the community crime control movement: 1) vigilanteism; 2) groups will attempt to exclude racial and/or ethnic minorities from neighbourhoods; 3) groups will become stridently anti-police in their attitudes and practices; and, 4) groups will adopt radical political ideologies.

Taking each in turn, there has not been a single incident of vigilanteism in any of the 100-or-so groups in Northeastern City since observation began in 1981. Vigilanteism remains a vary rare phenomenon in the United States. (This does not mean that anti-crime groups do not occasionally apprehend an offender and turn him/her over to the police; they do. But apprehension is not vigilantesim; vigilantism occurs when citizens attempt to punish someone they apprehend.)

The problem of excluding minorities has been discussed earlier. For the most part, groups are quite sophisticated in how they approach racial and ethnic problems. Nevertheless, the potential of such racism persists and occasionally can be observed camouflaged in a variety of ways. It seems probable that most groups are concerned about class rather than racial differences, having learned that working and middle class minorities share common neighbourhood and moral values with working and middle class whites.

Strident anti-police attitudes simply have not developed in anti-crime groups. They are often critical of police in ways described above. For the most part, however, criticism of police remains constructive and appropriate. This doesn't mean that criticisms of police are always correct; they are often not. It means instead that anti-crime groups, like consumer groups, review and evaluate services. The nature of their evaluations, right or wrong, should provide police with another important source of feedback about public perceptions of police performance. And, finally, community anti-crime groups simply have not been associated with radical politics.

Conclusion
The community crime control movement in the United States has demonstrated great potential to reduce or control crime, disorder, and fear. Community crime control groups succeed both through their own independent activities and by working in collaboration with police and other governmental and non-governmental agencies. The American experience does not suggest that independent groups veer towards vigilanteism, exclusion of minorities, anti-police activities, or radical political ideologies. For the most part, anti-crime groups, whether sponsored or not by police organizations, are constructive community organizations which provide powerful touch-points in communities for police. They can be testy, they place demands on police, but they are dedicated to peaceful and harmonious communities: the same goal of the police. Whether the community anti-crime movement has the same potentials, with as few dangers, in other political circumstances remains to be seen.

9 Trends in Canadian crime prevention

Patricia Brantingham

Using an analogy from preventive medicine, crime prevention activities can be divided into primary, secondary and tertiary measures (Brantingham and Faust, 1976). Primary crime prevention identifies conditions in the physical *and* social environments that facilitate criminal acts and alters those conditions. Secondary crime prevention identifies potential offenders (i.e. individuals at risk), and intervenes in their lives to keep them from committing offences. Tertiary crime prevention keeps people who have already committed crimes from committing further crimes in the future. Under this broad definition almost anything done within the criminal justice system can be considered crime prevention, from the incapacitation of the criminal to the police patrol.

In Canada the term *crime prevention* is usually, though not exclusively, associated with primary crime prevention activities. These can be divided into those designed to reduce opportunities to commit offences and those activities intended to address the socio-economic causes of crime (Clarke, 1981). Opportunity reduction techniques have always existed. While the crime prevention movement of the 1970s emphasized opportunity reduction. (Canadian Association of Chiefs of Police, 1975), it did not invent locks, bars, walls or vigilance over possessions. The crime prevention movement *did* make opportunity reduction the basis of formal government programmes through which individuals were helped to protect their own property.

Similarly, programmes intended to alter the socio-economic conditions thought to 'cause' crime have been around for a long time in Canada and elsewhere. The Chicago Area project, begun in the 1930s and made famous by Shaw and McKay (1969), is the quintessential social prevention programme in North America. The project sought, and still seeks, to develop methods to alter the behaviour of juvenile delinquents and prevent delinquency. Burgess's 1937 description of the Chicago Area Project sounds remarkably similar to descriptions of social prevention programmes developed in the 1980s:

> "All of the activities in the programme are carried on with the view to making the neighbourhood conscious of the problems of delinquency, collectively interested in the welfare of its children, and active in promoting programmes for such improvement of the community environment as will develop in the children interests and habits of a constructive and socially desirable character." (Burgess, Loham, and Shaw, 1937.)

103

At the same time while the crime prevention movement of the 1970s included both forms of primary crime prevention, many of which were remarkably similar to the Chicago Area Project, the emphasis has been on opportunity reduction (Normandeau and Hasenpusch, 1978). However there is a growing trend for crime prevention to move back toward the social work, recreational educational approaches which developed out of the 'child-saving' movement of the turn of the century. There are some exceptions to this, two of which are described in this chapter.

Institutional development of crime prevention in Canada

The most comprehensive government support for crime prevention in Canada is provided by the Ministry of the Solicitor General. This Ministry has functional responsibility for the police, prisons and the treatment of offenders. In addition to its main tasks, the Ministry funds training and conferences; provides a network of regional criminal justice consultants; and supports research and documents model programmes (good practice). Through its funding and policy statements, the Ministry has had a major impact on the evolution of crime prevention in Canada.

The police have been the primary organizers of crime prevention programmes. Local policing is provided by municipal police forces in many cities and towns or, under contract, by provincial police forces in many communities in Ontario and Quebec, and by the Royal Canadian Mounted Police (RCMP) in other provinces and the territories. The RCMP also serves as a national police force with powers and responsibilities somewhat similar to those of the American Federal Bureau of Investigation.

The RCMP, with its national scope and clearly defined administrative hierarchy, has well-developed crime prevention policies and provides an integrated core for police sponsored crime prevention activities. Municipal police forces have supported crime prevention programmes to varying degrees.

Ten years ago, most police executives in Canada resisted the idea of funding crime prevention activities. They saw 'real' police work as enforcing the law and catching criminals, not as preventing crime. When crime prevention units first began to appear in police departments, the constables who were assigned to them tended to regard the assignment as punishment for some failure at 'real' police work. Constables who were poor drivers were often assigned to crime prevention. Promotions came from 'real' police work, not crime prevention activities.

Over the past decade, crime prevention has become more readily accepted in Canadian policing. The duties of constables assigned to newly formed crime prevention units vary from place to place and province to province, but in general, they involve both crime prevention and community relations activities. Crime prevention duties typically involve setting up prevention programmes, speaking to groups and carrying out security checks. The RCMP have headquarters staff dedicated to crime prevention activities on a full-time basis and operate a national crime prevention training programme. The uniformity of training tends to produce a relatively consistent pattern of police sponsored crime prevention programmes across Canada. Crime prevention practitioners' associations have been formed by crime prevention officers to develop their own support networks. Prevention is even beginning to be seen as a base for career advancement within the police. At least one chief of police in a major Canadian city has recently been promoted to his post from a crime prevention/community relations unit.

Crime prevention is likely to continue to be an important approach to crime control within Canadian policing. Although not yet universally recognized as 'real' police work in all Canadian forces, it is now generally accepted by most forces. Government sponsorship and funding of crime prevention, while threatened by tight budgets in some places, seems fairly secure. The only thing currently in doubt is which activities ought to be seen as falling under the 'crime prevention' mantle in the future.

Core programmes
The programmes and activities which fall under the title *crime prevention* are changing. There are, however, three approaches that have been tried in most Canadian cities.

(i) Community surveillance
The best known crime prevention programme in North America is *neighbourhood watch* or *block watch*. In this programme the police attempt to reduce the amount of crime in a neighbourhood by alerting its residents to the presence of crime and by convincing them that they should 'watch' what goes on around them and report any suspicious activity. The programme rests on the assumption that the police patrol is comparatively ineffective in providing protective surveillance in residential areas, and on the complementary belief that residents can act as pervasive, natural, unobjectionable watchers and guardians.

Neighbourhood watch has fathered a series of variants: marine watch in marinas and harbours; realtor's watch for empty houses; business watch; taxi watch; and surveillance by bus drivers.

(ii) Property marking
Property marking is usually carried through a programme called *Operation Identification*. Property is marked with the owner's unique identifier. Decals indicating that property within a dwelling or building has been marked are usually displayed on a window or door. The theory behind this programme is obvious: marked goods are supposed to be more difficult to dispose of by criminals and easier to identify when used in evidence; the decal warns the potential thief of the enhanced risk involved in stealing from that building and the thief goes elsewhere.

(iii) Target hardening
In target hardening, physical barriers are used to protect property: detectors on clothes in department stores; locks; bars on windows; alarms; steering wheel locks on cars; safes for narcotics in pharmacies. Barriers make specific crimes more difficult, if not impossible to commit.

Target hardening is a prominent and continually growing approach to crime prevention. Police security survey programmes quite naturally tend to suggest target hardening solutions to building security problems. In addition, there is a rapidly growing private security and alarm industry. The target hardening approach, of course, obviously predates the recent crime prevention movement. Much of Canada's most entertaining fiction over the years has involved the technical battle of wits between target hardeners and thieves.

Additional programmes
Along with the core programmes, many additional programmes have been tried under the banner of crime prevention. These range from counselling first-time juvenile offenders (for a review, see Rowe, 1981; Rowe and Edelman, 1982) to police dressing in cute animal costumes in order to make themselves more acceptable to the young.

Some of the more interesting programmes involve offering the services of trained volunteers, for example, accompanying the elderly on errands or providing escort in the evening. Such services work more at reducing fear of victimisation than actual victimisation. The danger with these volunteer programmes, of course, is that they could develop into *ad hoc* volunteer patrols and vigilante groups.

Many of the programmes are designed to address juvenile crime, particularly vandalism and theft. Media campaigns are used to attempt to convince juveniles that shop-lifting or vandalism are crimes. In one community in Ontario, the police used community committees and peer pressure to reduce school vandalism. In this programme the municipal government gave local schools a budget for films. All vandalism repair costs came out of that budget. Vandalism meant fewer films. The programme reported a 40 per cent drop in school vandalism in the first year.

Crime prevention programmes have been designed to educate individuals and groups, especially children; to counsel high-risk persons and families of potential or first-time offenders; to provide activities for teenagers; to persuade through the media; to influence community activities through police/community councils; and to teach through documentation of model programmes. In sum, the core crime prevention programmes in Canada are police based, *primary* prevention programmes. The other programmes usually involve community groups working with the police as a resource or as an organising force and frequently are *secondary* or *tertiary* crime prevention programmes.

The current state of North American crime prevention:
doubts and policy shifts
In the 1970s and early 1980s, the growth in crime prevention was primarily institutional; that is the growth of police support for crime prevention and police-based programmes. At the same time research was directed at identifying and proving the worth of specific crime prevention efforts. In the United States, the Federal

Government funded major research projects such as the environmental design projects in Portland, Oregon (follow-up study by Kushmuk and Whittemore, 1981), and in Hartford, Connecticut (Gardiner, 1978; Fowler and Mangione, 1982), or the community redevelopment project in the Midwood section of Brooklyn, a New York suburb (Abt Associates, 1980).

The hope was that major projects would uncover fundamental casual relationships that could be used to develop general crime prevention approaches which could be used as blueprints to reduce crime in many communities. Implicit in the funding of large model projects, and the move towards standardised programmes such as block watch or operation identification was the assumption that crime is a fairly simple phenomenon or, at least, one that does not vary much from place to place.

Crime prevention research was also undertaken in Canada, but not on the same scale as in the United States or in England. Research was and is funded both federally through the Ministry of the Solicitor General, or its network of regional consultants, and provincially through the various provincial ministries of the Attorney General's Department and universities.

While some programmes have been successful (see Normandeau and Hasen- pusch, 1978 for a general summary; see Worrell, 1984 for an example of a success- ful neighbourhood watch programme), many others have failed (see Hackler, 1978; Normandeau and Hasenpusch, 1978). The 1980s have seen the acceptance of a more sophisticated view of crime prevention; similar programmes, ones which can be expected to succeed in one community may fail in others; work for one type of crime, but not for others. For example, block watch and neighbourhood watch schemes are based on developing the willingness of persons living in the same area to watch the property of others living in that area; their ability to watch for unusual activity; their willingness to call the police if they see something that appears to be 'wrong'. Persons not only have to be willing to watch, they have to be able to watch. Block watch programmes will fail if those areas where residents are not wil- ling to watch *or* if they cannot watch. In areas where there are strong social norms against interferring, or where few people are home, or where people cannot watch because bushes or fences block sight-lines, or because traffic noise forces them to withdraw within their houses, block watch will not work. Even in areas where people are able to watch, crime may well be such a rare event and the individual risk of victimisation low, most people will stop watching after a while.

Areas within cities differ. Residents' perceptions of problems differ. The capacities of local areas to deal with crime differ. Responses to crime differ (Podolefsky, 1983; Lavrakas and Herg, 1982; McPherson, 1982; Brantingham, *et al* 1979). It is most unlikely therefore that a 'core' programme could be devised that would work in all situations. There is a growing awareness that crime prevention efforts must be flex- ible, adaptable, based on assessments of crime problems at the local level and based on the capacity of a community to respond to a crime problem. This form of crime prevention can be seen best in the policies and actions of the Ministry of the Solicitor General and the environmental design efforts of the RCMP in British Columbia.

Ministry of the Solicitor General

Because the Ministry of the Solicitor General has national responsibility and national scope, policy shifts have clear impact. As early as 1979, Ministry officials were writing about the importance of linking responsibility for crime prevention to the specifics of the crime problem and the nature of the community resources (Engstad and Evans, 1979). By 1983, the Ministry had developed a crime prevention policy that supported community-based, flexible crime prevention programming.

The approach of the Ministry of the Solicitor General is interesting at two levels: it reflects, in an integrated manner, the general trend away from standard off-the-shelf 'core' programmes and the movement towards using the police as a resource, not as the providers of crime prevention. It moves crime prevention policy away from programmes and towards a process. The Ministry is now developing a national network of community associations and special interest groups willing to work on crime prevention. Members of the network, called *Canadians for Crime Prevention,* do several things: they help in the design and implementation of a National Crime Prevention Week through provincial planning groups. They also serve as a vehicle for the distribution of crime prevention information and for instituting locally based crime prevention programmes.

The Ministry of the Solicitor General is developing an approach to crime prevention in which it nurtures an information network, tries to get community groups rather than individuals interested in crime prevention but does not dictate how community groups should respond.

British Columbia

The RCMP in British Columbia are carrying out perhaps the most innovative police sponsored crime prevention effort in Canada if not in North America. Policing in the cities, towns and rural areas of British Columbia is, to a large extent, provided by detachments of the RCMP working under contract rather than by municipally controlled police forces. Some four years ago, the RCMP began an active programme of training their crime prevention officers in techniques of prevention through environmental design. Through their training academy, the RCMP developed a course for crime prevention officers that teaches the basic approaches in situational crime prevention, particulary as applied to the review of development plans and town planning decisions.

The crime prevention officers receive training both in the theory underlying environmental criminology and in the methods and processes for applying situational crime prevention analysis in building design reviews and town planning decisions. In essence, the crime prevention officers are trained to identify design features that might make commission of various types of crime easy. The officers look for target-specific characteristics such as the juxtaposition of a highly vulnerable building with a location that might attract potential offenders, as well as area-specific characteristics such as lack of access control.

When they return to their detachments, these trained crime prevention officers make contact with local planners; sit on advisory design panels and advisory community planning committees; and, generally, provide crime prevention input into development decisions.

The RCMP input into local planning decisions includes encouraging diversion of traffic in order to reduce nuisances in residential neighbourhoods; suggesting designs for street layouts in new subdivisions in order to reduce the flow of potential offenders; planning parking at shopping centres in order to increase natural surveillance; and suggesting designs for apartment buildings to increase security.

In the relatively short time since the training programme was initiated, these trained crime prevention officers have influenced decisions on projects ranging from the design of a harbour front redevelopment, to the design of a complete new town. Description of two of these projects in instructive.

In 1984, the municipality of Port Alberni began a harbourside redevelopment. Port Alberni is a small city located on the coast of Vancouver Island. Its economy is based on three sectors; forestry, commercial fishing and fish processing, none of which is expected to grow in the near future. Port Alberni's location amid the rugged scenic beauty of the coast makes it a natural tourist stop. In an attempt to increase tourism, the municipality, together with the federal and provincial government, began a project intended to redevelop a segment of the city's waterfront for tourism. The project has several parts: tourist information centre, exhibition space, a pier with an observation deck from which to view the fishing fleet, a park, a snack bar and an observation tower. The cost of the initial phase of the project was over $2 million (see, Canada-British Columbia TIDSA, 1983).

The local RCMP detachment's crime prevention officer was asked to review the project. The police made a number of suggestions for modifications to project plans to reduce criminal opportunities (see, Hest and Harrison, 1983). The assessment of the development plans and the recommendations made provide a good illustration of the British Columbia approach to situational crime prevention.

The first step in the review was a thorough analysis of local crime. The area was found to have an extremely high rate of calls for police service, about five per building per year. The calls for service were mostly related to drinking offences and associated nuisance behaviour, and to minor property offences including vandalism and theft. The area has many pubs and bars. The crime prevention officers concluded that there was no reason to expect that a new tourist attraction in the area would reduce the demand for police services.

The crime prevention officers next analysed the proposed development on the basis of the existing problems in the area and the projected increase in the flow of people through the area. Specifically, they looked at parking and traffic related problems and the potential for vandalism and theft. They identified what they believed to be specific problems such as:

— a five-way uncontrolled intersection (traffic accident potential);

— poor levels of lighting in certain parts of the area (vandalism potential in an area that already experiences high levels of vandalism);

— lack of any surveillance potential, official or unofficial, in some places (vandalism, theft, and break and entry potential);

— danger from adjacent industrial structures, particularly an unfenced fuel tank storage area (the new development would cut off access to the fire boat if there were a fire in the fuel storage area);

— free access and the encouragement of tourists to wander near the fire boat, police boat, and pilot boat (vandalism and minor theft potential).

Based on the crime analysis and problem indentification, the crime prevention officers suggested a series of changes to the development plans. The design suggestions included: traffic lights or, at a minimum, some pedestrian crossing zone at the five-way intersection; more lighting on a pathway; the elimination of an earth mound that obstructed surveillance potential; and controlled access to the pier area, particularly near the police boat and the fire boat. In working with city officials, the crime prevention officers were able to implement about half of the changes.

In the second project the crime preventive officers of the RCMP worked with the provincial government and with private consultants in the developing of a new coal town in north-eastern British Columbia. Situational crime prevention analysis was integrated into the process of designing the town and suggestions for changes in potentially crime generating design features were made at several junctures. The crime, safety and nuisance potentials of commercial, institutional and residential designs were considered. Crime potential was, of course, only one consideration for the design team, and crime potential was not always the consideration that 'won out' when several different design considerations conflicted. The situational crime prevention suggestions put to the architects and planners for the new town included:

— redesign of some pedestrian paths, particularly paths for children, to create natural routes from home to school or to the city centre (reduce vandalism and nuisance behaviour);

— redesign of layout for the public and the pub's parking lot to segregate pub parkers from shoppers' automobiles. The crime prevention team also suggested the use of canned rather than bottled beer (reduce vandalism and nuisance problems);

— inclusion of special attractions at the town's recreation centre together with the reduction of attractions in the shopping area in order to draw teenagers to the recreation centre and away from the town centre. In particular, a special video games area with video games that operate on token rather than coins was added to the recreation centre and a proposed commercial video arcade was deleted from the town centre plan (reduce potentials for shoplifting, vandalism, littering and nuisance behaviour);

– inclusion of a 24 hour taxi office, situated to overlook and therefore provide a natural surveillance of a parking lot (reduce potentials for vandalism and car theft);

– inclusion of a cafeteria in the high school to keep teenagers on campus at lunch time (reduce shoplifting potential in the town centre);

– redesign of some roadways and elimination of an apartment building to allow natural movement of secondary school students to and from the town centre (reduce vandalism and theft potentials).

As with the Port Alberni project, not all recommendations were accepted by the design team.

The pattern of recommendations in these projects is typical of recommendations made in other British Columbia crime prevention projects. The approach followed by the police involves designing access routes that minimize the potential for conflict and crime; an emphasis on reducing minor offences and nuisance behaviour; and an attempt to displace potentially criminal or nuisance behaviour into less obnoxious forms of behaviour or to less vulnerable, or at least apparently less vulnerable locations.

Assessing the effectiveness of crime prevention work is difficult. However, limited and local crime prevention effects have already been demonstrated, and within several years it should be possible, using a new RCMP crime reporting system, to estimate the general result of planned change on reported crime. Such an analysis will be complex, of course, because local effects will have to be separated from global effects. Displacement is always a possibility, and while the displacement of crime through a planning intervention has target-specific value, it has no overall value unless it takes the form of displacement from more serious forms of criminal behaviour to a less serious form.

The future
The 1980s have seen a greater understanding of the complexity of a crime (Brantingham and Brantingham, 1984; Conklin, 1981) and a move towards situational responses to crime problems (see, Clarke and Mayhew, 1980). Crime prevention is beginning to invlove the detailed analysis of the specific crime problem, an analysis of the social and physical environment in which crime occurs, and an assessment of the capacity of official agencies, community groups and individuals to respond. Crime prevention is becoming a process, not a set of programmes. This approach (illustrated in the two projects described above) while offering the potential to reduce crime in a way in which standard, off-the-shelf programmes cannot, has a number of problems. This is to be expected. If a teachers' association

111

becomes involved in crime prevention, it should not be surprising that the association sees educational solutions to crime problems. If church groups get involved, it is natural to expect that decreasing moral standards are seen as a problem. Groups sponsoring recreational programmes see lack of recreation as a problem leading to crime. Problems are defined by the solutions. Solutions are defined, in part, by knowledge, experience and preferences.

With community groups and associations pursuing their own interests and expertise in defining crime prevention programmes, the field of crime prevention begins to move back towards the social work, educational, and recreational approaches that predated the opportunity reduction oriented crime prevention movement of the 1970s.

Two community projects in Canada are perhaps representative of the type of projects that are likely to develop and dominate during the next ten years. The West Island YMCA in Montreal, Quebec, became involved in direct crime prevention in 1974. The YMCA set up a group of community/volunteer based programmes designed for 'hard to reach' young people. The programmes include supervising community work, teaching 'life-skills' and motorcycle riding, and group discussion programmes for school dropouts to stimulate educational interests and self-esteem. In addition, the association organises neighbourhood watch programmes and presents informational programmes about security.

A second project begun in 1981 by the University College of Cape Breton, Nova Scotia, attempted to develop community leadership and community crime prevention initiatives. This project takes an adult education approach and tries to teach community groups about crime and crime prevention and tries to link interested community groups with resources and information. Future plans will move the project into aid for associations or groups who have programmes for offenders. Both of these projects, the University College of Cape Breton project and the Montreal YMCA project, have strong community boards of directors with some support from police. Both these projects are moving toward secondary and tertiary sectors of prevention.

There are dangers in the shift towards social prevention and community-based crime prevention projects. Effective crime prevention requires an understanding of the crime problem and the ability to design flexible responses. If the movement in crime prevention continues away from the police, the ability to analyse the crime problem may be lost. The programmes which are designed may depend more on the participants' enthusiasms than on the nature of the crime problems they are intended to address. In cases such as these, responses to crime end up not reflecting the crime problem, but the interests of the community groups.

10 Welfare and Criminality in Sweden

Bo Svensson

"Criminality is a serious social problem which must be attacked on a broad front. One should not overestimate the significance of the measures that can be taken by the judiciary. The question must be viewed in a considerably broader perspective.

By continuing the work of building a more just society with greater equality we can eliminate many reasons for crime. It is particularly important to provide good conditions within which children and young people may grow up and find a position in society. By active measures in housing and family policies, in schools, working life and recreational activities, we can counteract social drop-out and take active responsibility for those afflicted by social and personal problems".

The above quotation, translated from the Fiscal Bill, for the financial year 1985–6, submitted to the Swedish Parliament in January 1985, reflects the conventional argument that the way to reduce crime is to increase the level of welfare provision. It is however an argument which, while finding support from time to time both in European countries and North America, has rarely been examined in any detail.

The Institute of Social Research in Stockholm, conducts regular surveys into living conditions throughout Sweden. The latest report "Welfare in the process of change: living conditions in Sweden" covering the period 1968–81, provided information on trends for a number of socio-economic characteristics which many would argue to have a direct bearing on crime rates. This chapter, which draws on the report, compares trends in welfare provision with crime figures. The conclusions reached cast some doubts on the soundness of conventional thinking.

Welfare in the process of change
Employment
In comparison with other countries Sweden's level of employment is high. It was among the highest in the Organisation for Economic Co-operation and Development area in 1960 and since then has continued to rise faster than in other countries; it stood at 79.4 per cent of the population aged 15–64 years in 1980. The average figure for the entire OECD area in that year was 65.1 per cent.

One of the more signifcant trends since the end of the 60s is the continued rise of employment among women. Of all women aged 20–64 years 56 per cent were gainfully employed in 1968. By 1981 the figure had risen to 77 per cent. For men in the same age group the degree of employment has throughout been around 90 per cent.

Working Conditions
Many dirty, heavy jobs disappeared during the 70s through the decline of industrial and agricultural employment; and through expansion within the service section, the number of monotonous jobs with low educational requirements has also decreased. At the same time the employees freedom has increased in the work place: 74 per cent of all employees can now determine for themselves their pace of work, while the possibilities of telephoning and receiving visits at one's place of work have increased in most sectors.

Income
The average gross income, expressed in the 1980 monetary value, increased from SEK 48,300 in 1967 to 56,400 in 1980. The average income, after tax, rose from SEK 34,200 to 38,000 during the same period. At the same time the distribution of income in Sweden has become more equitable. Earlier studies point to a great equalisation of incomes during the 30s and 40s, and a relatively stable distribution up to the end of the 60s, after which there appears to have been a further move towards equalisation. Comparative studies, suggest that by the end of the 1960s Sweden had a more equitable distribution of income than most other OECD countries rivalled only perhaps by Holland. As Figure 10.1 shows this trend has continued.

Education
During the period 1967–81 there was a considerable increase in the level of educational provision. This applied both to ordinary schooling, in which increasing numbers of pupils continued to higher education; to study circles and to training courses in working hours. While there continues to be variation between one socio-economic group and the next in the amount of education received, these differences are diminishing, the overall trend in the numbers receiving education and the amount of education received is increasing (Figure 10.2).

Housing standards
Before the war housing conditions in Sweden were among the worst in Europe but they improved rapidly throughout the post-war period. In 1966 the regulations regarding acceptable housing standards were revised with the result that 1,675,000 persons were considered to be living in overcrowded conditions. New standards specified that there should be at most two persons per room, not counting kitchen and living room, and the rent of a new three-room flat (the normal accommodation for a family with two children) should not exceed 20 per cent of the average industrial wage. By 1968 the country was in the midst of its 'million programme': one million flats were to be built between 1965 and 1974. The result of the programme was dramatic. In 1968 almost every fifth household was overcrowded, in 1974 less than one-tenth, and in 1981 just over 3 in a 100. The majority of all households now meet a generous space standard; all persons in these households have at least one room apart from kitchen and living-room.

114

Figure 10.1   Development of equality of incomes 1951 to 1980

The maximal equalisation coefficient; MU (percentage of the total sum of incomes which
would need to be transferred from those with incomes above the median income to those
below it for all to have an equal income)
Source: Valfard i ferandring

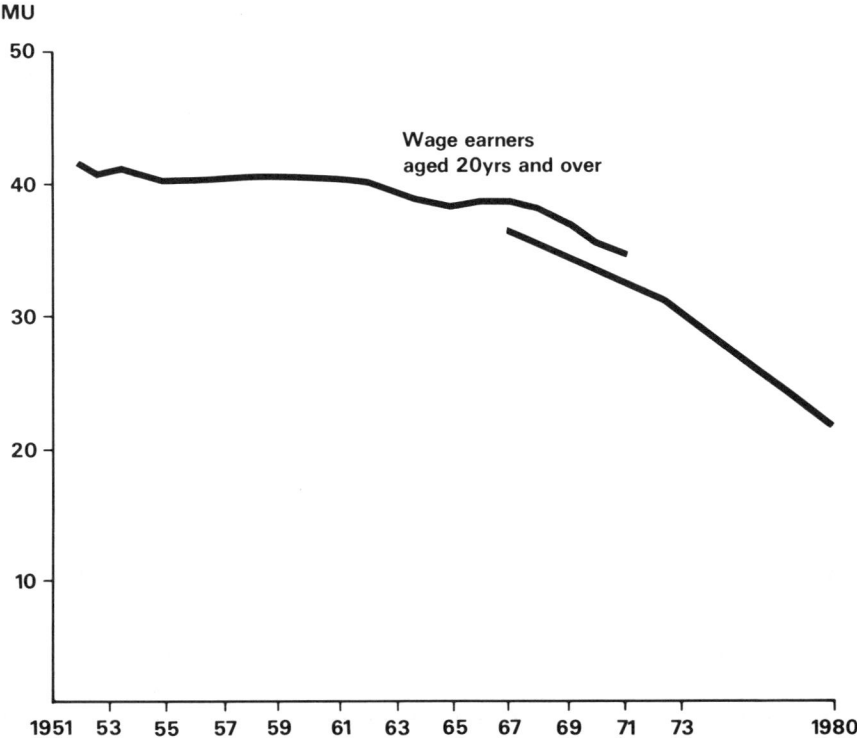

Family structure and stability
By the end of the 1960s the number of divorces had increased, while the number
of marriages had decreased. At the same time it became increasingly common for
people to live together without getting married, with the result that the family
flourishes albeit in a new form. The figure of married and/or cohabiting persons
is thus largely unchanged, about 65 per cent of the population in the period 1968–81.
The nuclear family as well (cohabitants and married couples with children) continues.
In important respects therefore the anchorage in family life remained unchanged
between 1968 and 1981.

Recreational activity
During the period between 1968 and 1981 people's leisure appears to have been
enriched or at least more organised. Occupations of the past such as reading
weekly magazines, wandering the streets and motoring trips have become less

115

Figure 10.2   Mean length of education in different groups of cohorts who have completed their education

Source: Valfard i ferandring

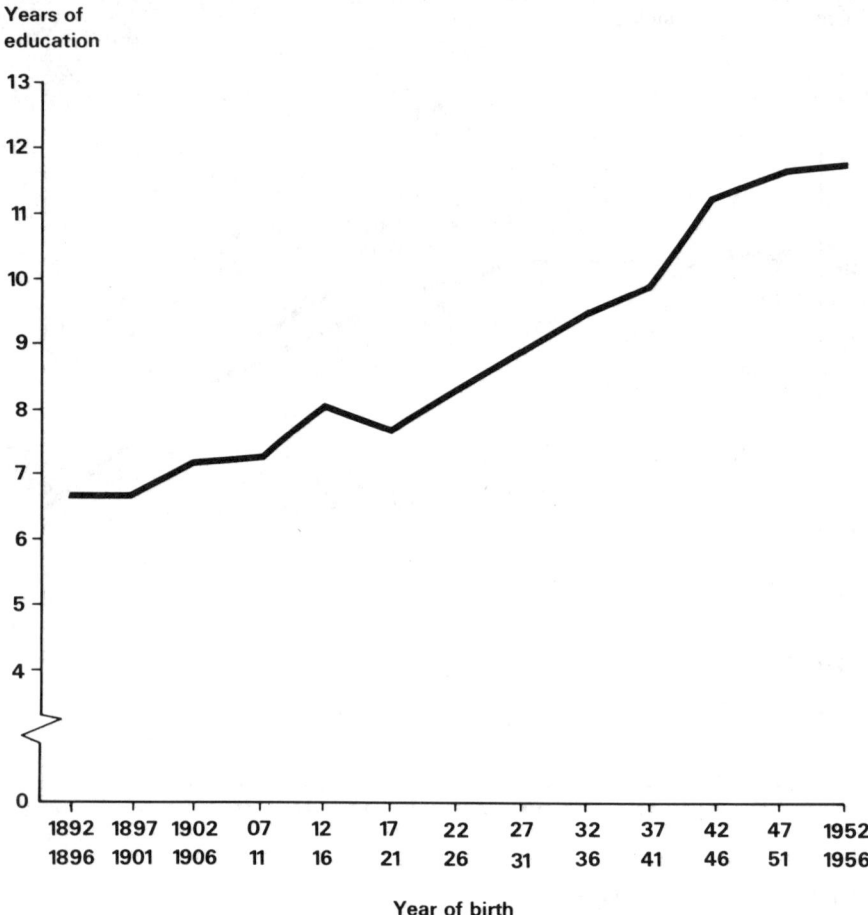

Year of birth

popular, while outdoor activities, and cultural activities have increased. The differences between occupational groups have in general diminished.

The picture in Sweden, despite covering the period of a world oil and economic crisis is predominantly bright. From 1968 to 1981 the proportion of the population having problems stemming from inadequate welfare provision has been substantially reduced.

The crime trend

Statistics on crimes brought to the notice of the police have been kept since 1950. Owing to various sources of error it is impossible to make any precise statement about actual criminality. Thus only a proportion of crimes come to the notice of the authorities, and the reporting process is affected, among other things, by the visibility of crime, the extent of damage, the social relations between victim and offender, and the action by the authorities.

Despite the limitations of official figures the view is generally held in Sweden that they provide an acceptable overall picture of the actual trend. Figure 10.3 shows the numbers of reported and cleared-up crimes against the Penal Code from 1950 to 1983.

Figure 10.3   Crimes in thousands 1950 to 1983

   I. All reported crimes against the Penal Code.
  II. Reported crimes against property.
III. Reported crimes against the person.

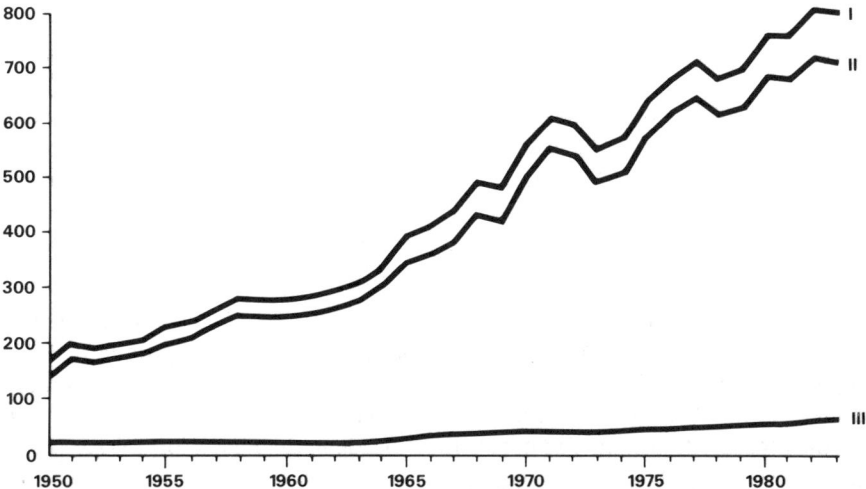

Between 1968 and 1981, that is the period covered by the standard-of-living studies reported above, the number of crimes against the Penal Code (I) rose from 494,000 in 1968 to 761,000 in 1981, or by 54 per cent. This trend which cannot be explained by population change, is accounted for primarily by an increase in the number of crimes against property (II). These crimes, which make up 90 per cent of crimes against the Penal Code, increased during the period from 435,000 in 1968 to 683,000 in 1981, or by 57 per cent.

Crimes against persons (III) which increased by 50 per cent during the period, constitute, at 7 per cent, a comparatively small proportion of crimes against the Penal Code.

Crimes of violence in Sweden are highly related to drunkenness. The Swedish research indicates that between 70–80 per cent of the offenders and 40–50 per cent of the victims are under the influence of alcohol at the time of such crimes. Measures have been taken therefore to reduce alcohol consumption in the hope that crime would fall. Alcohol sales in 1983 were 20 per cent below the 1976 level (6.1 against 7.7 litres of pure alcohol per inhabitant). Figures of illicit distilling during the same period are not available, but support for the view that alcohol consumption has *actually* diminished comes from the fact that the number of cases of cirrhosis of the liver has also diminished. The changed alcohol habits are, however, not yet reflected in the police statistics for crimes of violence.

It is also the case that the continued growth of welfare during the period 1968–81 has not been associated with lower levels of crime. Indeed, the increased welfare has been achieved by reorganisation of production which in turn has led to new forms of consumption and, at the same time, appears to have increased the opportunities for crime.

The opportunity structure

According to the statistics – which are considered to be reliable for this type of crime – thefts were 4–5 times higher in 1983 than in 1950. What lies behind this development? To answer that question it is necessary to broaden the perspective and study theft over a longer period. There are no national statistics of crimes coming to the notice of the police for the period prior to 1950. There are, however, statistics, since 1830, of convicted persons. These give a rough picture of criminality. The trend as regards cases of larceny appears from Figure 10.4

This shows that the number of persons convicted of theft has varied greatly over the past 150 years. In the mid-19th century Sweden was a poor developing country in which crimes of theft were common. That poverty was an important factor is apparent from the figures for 1867 and 1868. In those years there were crop failures which gave rise to a wave of thefts. Food shortage was probably the reason for the high figure also in 1918 during the blocade in the First World War.

The falling figures in the second half of the 19th century can therefore be attributed to the growing welfare following in the steps of industrialisation, which put an end to the criminality of the destitute in our country.

In the 20th century, however, the criminality of the destitute has been superseded by what may be called welfare criminality. The trend describes a S-curve. It starts slowly in the first two decades, increases in the interwar period, reaches a peak in the 50s, when it also reaches its turning point, thereafter continuing at a slower rate in the 60s. If this is a correct reflection of the true trend, the forecast – with unchanged criminal policy – points to a levelling off and a relatively stable level in the 80s.

This trend can be considered in relation to a number of important societal changes; first, the exodus from the countryside into the anonimity of the towns is associated with higher criminality.

Today more than 75 per cent of all women are estimated to have gainful employment outside the home. This development has meant that people are forced to

Figure 10.4 Prosecution for Larceny 1831–1980 (5 year means)

Logarithmic Scale.
Source: Van Hofer & Thamo Stold i Sverige 1931–1980
(Thefts in Sweden 1931–1980)

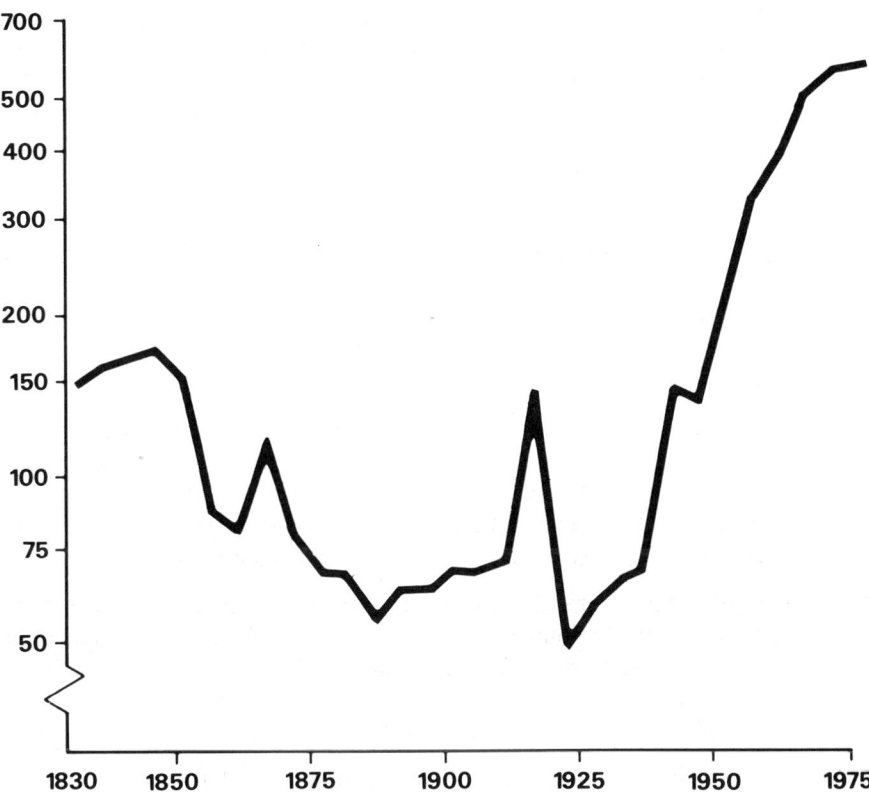

Number of
prosecutions
per 100,000 inh.

leave their possessions without supervision. The houses of married couples, both of whom are at work, and of single persons with a job, are left empty all day. To be a thief in Sweden today has become an 9–5 job.

Some of the increase in general welfare has led to a growth in the number of summer cottages which stand empty perhaps 300 days a year. And when they are inhabited the town flat is empty. The Burglary Division of the Stockholm Police has its peak season when Stockholmers return from their holidays and find their homes plundered.

Among other things, increased welfare has been won by an increase in efficiency in the job market involving the reduction or complete disappearance of many traditional occupations, some of which had an important crime prevention function. For example, the demise of personal service in favour of self-service in shopping. Despite largely the same clientele, there is a great difference in the extent of shop-lifting between the old-fashioned over-the-counter sales in the liquor retail shops and in today's supermarkets with their provocative display of goods.

Rising crime in Sweden today may also be ascribed to increased mobility. The improved communications, and especially the ownership of a car, have enorm-ously increased the opportunities for commission of crime. As many as one-third of all crimes against the Penal Code coming to the notice of the police in 1983 were thefts of, or from, cars and other vehicles and damage. No data exist of the number of crimes involving the use of a car, but they are undoubtedly many. The burglar and receiver need a car for carrying off the stolen goods, the robber for getting away with his booty. The significance of the motor-car for Swedish crimi-nality can hardly be overestimated.

The changes outlined have brought, above all, an increase in the supply of goods for private consumption. The number of valuable objects for theft has risen enormously. With improved technology many of them have also become smaller and easier to steal (transistorisation of radio and TV sets and the home computer are examples).

The fact that there is more to steal weakens social control in the broader sense. The increased availability of goods means that their social value is reduced, as it is so much easier to replace them. The surveillance and other protective arrange-ments diminish and the social reactions against theft lessen. The control and the opportunity structure have a reciprocal influence on one another.

It can be argued that governments, albeit unwittingly, make important decisions bearing on the extent of criminality when they choose whether the people shall have, in Bismarck's words "guns instead of butter". When the decision is made for example, to invest in heavy industry instead of the production of consumer goods, the decision is also made on a lower-level of crime against property.

To pursue this point, economic growth often presumes a mobile labour market in which people seek jobs in the towns. If the traditional labour force does not suf-fice, new groups are driven or lured into the labour market by means, for example, of changed taxation rules. Housewives become blue- or white-collar workers. As a result of this, as noted above, many houses are left without supervision, and are easy game for burglars. The price of economic growth can become increased criminality.

In a similar way attempts to achieve a more equitable distribution of income often lead to increased tax evasion owing to the marginal tax effects. The form of the taxation system decides the extent and forms of tax offences. The structure of the transportation system – public transport or private motor cars – decides the extent and form of traffic offences. The examples can be multiplied. Often it is a matter of choice between two evils – economic stagnation, uneven income distribution, a rigid transport apparatus, on the one hand, and certain forms of criminality on the other. Experience suggests that the interest in keeping crime down is pushed into the background in favour of short-term economic gains. Criminality is not regarded as so great a problem as to justify really effective countermeasures.

This is not to argue that there can be no effective measures against crime. This is by no means the case. But such measures must have their place within the framework of the general development of society.

In practice this often entails directed action to get to grips with clearly specified problems. Work by the British Home Office Research and Planning Unit provides a useful example. This takes its starting point from the situation within which selected crimes occur and prescribes countermeasures tailor-made according to the circumstances.

The approach has been adopted in Sweden, to improve security in hospitals, museums and factories. A valuable example of the genre is offered also by the advice issued by the Swedish Football Association in 1984 to match organisers. These stipulate, for instance, that the actual football stadium shall be designed so as to meet strict security requirements. Railings should be set up to prevent the standing public from falling forwards, and different sections of the grandstand should be bounded off to prevent free movement of spectators. But in addition the Association recommends that the visiting team supporters be kept separate from those of the home team. The crowd of supporters should be met outside the arena and escorted to the section of the stand assigned to them. After the match they should similarly be escorted directly out to the buses, while the home team supporters are kept back. The Association's recommendations also include training of a match speaker, so that he can calm the public if a state of agitation arises, and of referees and of team-captains – the latter, for instance, are enjoined to ensure that players do not, by word or gesture, provoke the public to violence.

Another example comes from the guidelines issued by the National Council for Crime Prevention for security of cash in transit. The Council recommends measures aimed at reducing the number of cash transits. A first step is the adoption of cashless routines which should be used to a greater extent that at present for payment of salaries, pensions, sickness benefits, *etc.* The gains thus made entail not only a reduction in the quantities of cash, but also avoidance of the hazardous accumulation of money that now takes place in banks, post offices and companies in preparation for salary and pension payments, etc. For the same reason it is important that these payments be spread over the month.

As a second step the Council proposes that the Bank of Sweden maintain a larger number of offices or banknote depots for supplying post offices and banks with notes. This presupposes that banknotes entering the depots can be directly placed in circulation again without first passing through the Bank of Sweden in Stockholm. To further reduce the banks' transport requirements they should be entitled to interest from the Bank of Sweden on amounts that they place in their own strongrooms instead of sending them to the Bank of Sweden. Decentralized storage of banknotes in this way would bring about a considerable reduction of the large flows of banknotes across the country.

Locally it should be possible to build up security transport systems covering the needs both of the banks and post offices and of the transport of shops' cash takings. Where transportation of cash cannot be avoided specific preventive measures are based on the recommended quantity of securities transported.

These guidelines have been followed by a special study of security cash bags. These bags are so designed that their contents are rendered unusable if attempts are made by an unauthorised person to open them. The system works in such a way that no action is necessary on the part of the carrier if subjected to attempted robbery; nor can the carrier open the bag while carrying it. A robber has then nothing to gain from threatening, injuring or forcing the carrier to accompany him.

There is a strong case for developing the preventive approach to crime and in doing so for ensuring that it rests not on conventional wisdom but on empirical observation, that is, a detailed study of the situations within which crime occurs. But further work in this area is also needed; in particular, we need to ensure that situational prevention does not merely displace offending in time or space. If these apprehensions can be satisfactorily dealt with, there will be nothing to prevent a complete change in the approach of the Swedish police.

11 Principles, issues and further action

Kevin Heal and Gloria Laycock

The last five years have seen increasing activity in crime prevention. Practitioners, including the police, social workers, probation officers and members of voluntary organisations now give greater practical weight to prevention than hitherto: criminologists are developing the theoretical ideas underlying prevention, while in Sweden, Canada, the Netherlands and the United Kingdom central governments are embracing crime prevention within the mainstream of their strategies against crime.

Activity and systematic reflection do not always go hand in hand, and the growth of crime prevention has brought with it many unanswered questions; what is the scope of crime preventive action? What are the pitfalls in developing this response to crime? Is the current interest likely to prove ephemeral or does it mark the development of a new and powerful aspect to deterrence within the criminal justice system?

Questions such as these will be easily answered with the benefit of hindsight, but neither the policy maker nor the practitioner facing the crime problems of the mid-1980s can enjoy such luxury. There is advantage, therefore, in standing back from the current round of initiatives, projects and schemes; from the rhetoric and aspirations, and indeed from the untutored scepticism, to reflect on the current state of crime prevention and give some thought to future action. The material commissioned for this book provides an opportunity to embark on such an exercise.

This chapter falls into three sections. The first considers some of the more important issues of principle to be addressed in deciding whether or not to continue to develop crime prevention. The conclusion is reached that there is considerable scope for preventive action against crime and that further work in this area is justified. The second section identifies some practical issues and finally, in the light of these discussions, a broad programme for the future development of prevention is outlined.

Issues of principle

Displacement of crime
There is little point in the policy maker investing resources and effort into situational prevention if by doing so he merely shuffles crime from one area to the next but never reduces it. For this reason the possibility of displacing crime by preventive intervention is a crucial issue for the policy maker. If substantial displacement

is inevitable, central governments, while having a responsibility to support and educate the individual who wishes to protect himself and his property, must look elsewhere in their bid to affect overall reductions of crime in society. If displacement is limited or non-existant then there is a case for greater investment in prevention since it will benefit the community at large and not simply the individual. What is the evidence about the displacement of crime?

Cornish and Clarke (Chapter 1) argue that criticism of situational crime prevention on the basis that it necessarily leads to displacement is an oversimplified view. It reflects the belief that criminal behaviour stems from an internalised criminal propensity or, to pursue the point, that crime is the product of "inter-psychic strife" or an aggressive response to frustrating events. Having listed several practical examples demonstrating that displacement is not an inevitable consequence of preventive intervention, Cornish and Clarke emphasise the rational decision making process associated with most, if not all, crimes. In this process the offender contemplates whether a particular criminal act will serve to meet some need (cash, social status, sexual gratification). His decision whether to commit a crime or not, or whether to commit it elsewhere or in some other form (both being forms of displacement) will be influenced by a range of factors including his existing value system; the likely benefits of the crime; the likelihood of being arrested and the opportunity to commit it somewhere else. The authors conclude that the more fully we understand the decision making process the more successful we will be in deciding whether a particular form of preventive intervention will lead to displacement.

The missing ingredient to the model proposed by Cornish and Clarke is some scale of readiness on the part of the individual to commit crime – some measure of the strength of his motivation. It must follow that displacement is more likely to take place where the individual's motivation is sufficiently high to drive him on even when his initial target of criminal activity is well defended. Where his motivation is lower, the protection of the target may well be sufficient to deflect the potential offender from crime altogether. At the same time, the range of alternative options open to him will probably affect his decision as to whether or not to adopt the criminal course of action.

In the chapter by Bennett (Chapter 4) the rational choice model is considered in the light of information gathered on the behaviour of burglars. Bennett argues that the *initial* decision whether to offend or not is socially or psychologically determined rather than situationally; however, the *final* decision as to whether to offend against a *particular* target is situationally determined. Thus while situational factors do not motivate the unmotivated, they will influence the final decision of the individual committed to offending. Bennett also provides strong support for the idea that motivation is not uncontrollable. He reaches a similar position to that reached on the base of the Cornish/Clarke analysis, namely that it is the characteristics of motivation – i.e. that motivation varies in strength from one offender to the next and is susceptible to control – which, together with the presence of a protected target, accounts for displacement. In supporting the situational response to crime Bennett acknowledges the difficulty of coping with those factors influencing the initial decision to commit crime but at the same time draws attention to those factors which can be controlled, and which may shape the final decision. Here he notes that locks are not particularly important as far as the offender is concerned but signs of occupancy are; similarly there is a concern with adjacent neighbours but little worry is caused by passers by.

We reach the position, therefore, that where the basic needs are weak, and the costs and risks of commiting the crime high, displacement is unlikely; however where the situation is reversed displacement may well occur.

On the basis of these arguments it would seem reasonable to suggest that situational prevention can reduce crime by influencing the final decision of some potential offenders, and that even where displacement takes place, only a proportion of the initial potential offenders will pursue their intent to commit crime.

Fear of crime
There is an argument that in order to promote crime prevention activity attention needs to be drawn to the problem of crime. If this argument is correct, and it almost certainly is, it raises the possibility of exacerbating the public's fear of crime, frequently without justification. One of the major difficulties in coping with this problem is that crime, and the fear of crime, are not homogeneously distributed across the population. This is clear from table 11.1. The task of promoting preventive activity in the inner city, or other high risk areas (where residents' fear of crime is justified), must be approached differently from that in rural or low risk areas where people are far more fearful than they need be.

In the inner cities it is likely that residents already have an accurate picture of the extent of crime; that fears are soundly based and the discussion of preventive measures will not exacerbate fear. Here the task is to convince people that crime can be reduced through their own activities, or in collaboration with other members of their community. There are examples in the United Kingdom, although at present they are rare, of neighbourhood watch schemes being established in high crime, inner city areas. Similarly there are claims of reductions in crime rates on high risk, local authority housing estates where a package of preventive measures (based on police, voluntary and local authority action) have been introduced. These may require a change in life style on the part of the individual e.g. locking doors, cancelling milk at holiday times etc.

In areas where crime rates are low but where the fear of crime remains high the task is different and, in some respects, more difficult. Here, through publicity and education, there is a need to counter the alarmist impression frequently given of crime by the local media, but, in doing so, to avoid creating a community complacent to the problems of crime. The message must be that crime is not out of control, and that sensible measures (which need not turn the home into a fortress) must be maintained for the continued well being of the community. Once good

125

Table 11.1 Burglary risks and fears, by Acorn neighbourhood group, 1983.

	Households burgled (including attempts) in 1983	Households burgled (excluding attempts) 1983	"Very worried" about burglary
	%	%	%
LOW RISK AREAS			
A. Agricultural areas (n = 476)	1	<1	10
C. Older housing of intermediate status (n = 2001)	2	1	18
K. Better-off retirement areas (n = 463)	3	1	17
J. Affluent suburban housing (n = 1659)	3	2	18
B. Modern family housing higher incomes (n = 1537)	3	2	20
MEDIUM RISK AREAS			
E. Better-off council estates (n = 1018)	4	2	25
D. Poor quality older terraced housing (n = 759)	4	3	29
F. Less well-off council estates (n = 1175)	4	2	31
HIGH RISK AREAS			
I. High status non-family areas (n = 609)	10	6	25
H. Multi-racial areas (n = 400)	10	6	36
G. Poorest council estates (n = 543)	12	7	41
NATIONAL AVERAGE	4	2	23

NOTES:
1. Weighted data; the Ns of each Acorn group are unweighted. Source: 1984 BCS.

2. Taken from 'Taking account of crime: key findings from the 1984 British Crime Survey' Hough and Mayhew (1985) Table 8, page 37.

crime prevention habits are established the fear will not be necessary for the maintenance of the behaviour. To draw an analogy with preventive medicine – it is not the constant fear of infection which leads to the washing of hands or food – it is habit.

The implication for the policy maker is that crime prevention must be tackled on a local basis. There are many reasons for tailoring the preventive programme to the local situation not least of which is the fact that crime rates will differ dramatically within and by area and this should be reflected in the approach adopted, particularly when steps are being taken to promote community action but alleviate fear.

The limits to preventive activity

Cornish and Clarke argue in their chapter that situational crime prevention has a role to play in the prevention of the majority of crimes, including crimes of violence. Trasler (Chapter 2), in contrast, takes the view that while situational crime prevention may be helpful in relation to acquisitive offending it is not applicable to the majority of expressive crimes. This is a relevant point of principle for the policy maker who needs to consider the scope for preventive activity. It is also necessary to identify the boundary, if there is one, between social and situational measures. Each is discussed below.

It is generally accepted that situational crime prevention has a useful contribution to make to the prevention of criminal damage or vandalism (Wilson, 1980; Sturman, 1980), burglary (Winchester and Jackson, 1982; Maguire, 1982; Laycock, 1984, 1985), shopcrime (Ekblom, 1986) and autocrime (Mayhew, *et al.*, 1980; Southall and Ekblom, 1985). Offences in these categories accounted for approximately 70% of crime recorded by the police in England and Wales during 1985. However, evidence of the effectiveness of situational prevention in relation to violence is limited although there is some support for the view that 'over the counter' robberies in Post Offices can be reduced through environmental measures. Moreover, robbery on the London underground system has been shown to be affected through the introduction of CCTV (Burrows, 1980), and aspects of street disorder are closely related to pub closing times (Ramsay, Chapter 7; Hope, 1985). Cornish and Clarke go further. They argue that in crimes of rape, wife battering and homicide, violence is *chosen* by the offender, with the implication that, had things (including the environmental setting) been different, the choice would have been otherwise. This analysis has considerable face validity – it makes sense. But it is particularly in relation to these more serious inter-personal offences of violence that the arguments put by Trasler apply. He maintains that situational crime prevention is less helpful in the control of this type of behaviour than the more traditional approaches (sentencing, incapacitation etc.).

While in theory Cornish and Clarke may be correct, in practice, and this is Trasler's point, the situation within which the decision to commit expressive crimes is taken, cannot readily be controlled and so does not offer a way of pre-empting the offence. The concern is, if the situation is relevant, can anything be done in practice to change it: could the offence be prevented? Here the answer, in most cases, is probably no. The theoretical discussion as to whether or not situational factors are relevant to the commission of the most extreme forms of violence is not the issue for the policy maker. Cornish and Clarke may prove to be correct in their arguments of the relevance of the situation to the generation of violent crime, but Trasler is almost certainly likely to be right in his assertion that expressive crimes are extremely difficult to prevent on any large scale through situational measures. In practice, situational crime prevention is probably most relevant to offences which can be shown to cluster in time or space and which are of a high rate (cf. Poyner, Chapter 3).

127

The final issue of principle to be discussed in this chapter concerns the balance to be struck between social and situational crime prevention measures. Social measures include attempts to revitalise the community through tenants groups, improve provision for youngsters' recreation etc. and by doing so strengthen the individuals' and communities' resolve against crime. Such measures are generally contrasted with situational measures for example, target hardening, or estate design. At first sight the two approaches are dissimilar; social crime prevention is seen as a liberal concept which is difficult to operationalise and focus, while situational prevention is frequently seen as a constraining activity, albeit one focussed directly on the reduction of crime. In practice the distinction is far from clear cut. For example, neighbourhood watch schemes are designed to increase surveillance and thereby increase the perceived risk to the offender in line with situational preventive ideas, but they clearly operate through the community and depend upon good relations for their existence. Other possible initiatives in social crime prevention may operate in a manner independent of situational variables; it is for research to explore the nature of these.

The successful development of prevention depends, therefore, not upon emphasising the differences between social and situational prevention, and pursuing each as if they were unrelated. Rather, ways need to be found of bringing the two approaches together and so ensuring that the measures developed within the context of situational crime prevention are acceptable to the community, have their support and, as a result, are implemented. As far as social measures are concerned the danger to be avoided is that they are deflected from the prevention of crime to other objectives which at best are only tangentially related to crime. As far as situational measures are concerned the danger to be avoided is that design and management measures aimed at reducing crime impair the quality of life for the individual member of the public and have an adverse effect on the appearance of our communities.

On the basis of the discussion so far it seems that the more obvious difficulties of principle associated with the development of prevention could be overcome. The question remains, however, as to whether it is *worth* taking the trouble to cope with these problems. As a first step in addressing this the next section looks at the costs of *not* taking preventive action.

Issues of practice

Protection of the individual
With the best will in the world it is not always possible for the individual to protect him or herself from crime. For example, it is extremely difficult for the individual to protect their car from theft or the house from burglary when the vulnerability stems from basic design faults. The optional extras now available for cars (eg crook locks and alarms) offer some protection, but the most sensible and cost effective solution is to be found in changes to the basic vehicle design. This requires action either by central or local government or national, professional or

commercial associations – i.e. the manufacturers themselves. It is not within the scope of individual action. The British Standard on vehicle security now being developed for England and Wales provides an example of a corporate approach to crime prevention aimed at the protection of the individual vehicle. Without this form of action at national level, action which is targetted at removing (rather than reducing) opportunities for crime, the individual would remain vulnerable or have to rely on manufacturers choosing to take action, voluntarily, on his behalf.

Protection of the weak
As Bayley (1980) has pointed out, the most advanced situational crime prevention is to be found in the protection of the property of the rich – both private and commercial: in the more expensive houses and flats rather than the properties on local authority housing estates where, in some areas, even the front door is insecure. Similarly, neighbourhood watch is more easily established in the middle class areas but has proved difficult to set up in the inner city where it is most needed. There are many other examples. Payment in cash (for wages or goods) is far more prevelant among the poor – so increasing their vulnerability to attack – than those with higher incomes where the use of credit cards, cheques and credit transfers gives a measure of protection against personal violence. It is also notable that motor manufacturers have only given serious consideration to prevention when designing the more expensive vehicles.

The concentration of situational measures among the affluent section of society is understandable, however, its effects may well be to drive criminal activity onto the most vulnerable. It has led to the criticism of situational crime prevention as likely to generate a fortressed middle class. Such a development is not inevitable, since there is almost certainly scope for extending situational measures against crime to other sectors of the community. For example, perhaps through voluntary sector organisations, some derivative of neighbourhood watch could be introduced to the inner city areas; the cost of improved designed-in security for private vehicles in the middle and lower price range is not as high as some manufacturers have suggested, and almost certainly within the budget of most customers (Southall and Ekblom, 1985); finally a small number of local authority housing departments have demonstrated that greater physical protection can be given to council tenants (Allatt, 1984). Again there is a need for a corporate or inter-agency, as opposed to an individual, response to crime prevention.

Trends in society
Finally, as Svensson notes in chapter 10, changes in life style, methods of production and consumer demands can increase the opportunities for crime. With more women working, and with holiday homes becoming more common, domestic property being unattended for longer periods of the day becomes more vulnerable to burglary. As Svensson notes, burglary becomes a 9-5 job. Similarly the opportunities for crime grow as the miniaturised consumer goods and portable electrical equipment such as TV sets or computers become fashionable and industry responds. Such goods are easily stolen and readily disposed of by the thief. Next,

the rationalisation of employment (which has come to mean the introduction of new technology and the slimming down of the workforce) takes no account of the surveillance traditionally provided by employees (store keepers; doormen; car park attendants). This, in turn, means that criminal opportunities are increased still further.

The solutions to each of these difficulties are different. On some occasions technological solutions may prove helpful. For example, with personal computers or even hi-fi equipment, it is technically possible to personalise the goods (e.g. through the incorporation of individual computer-type codes) to the extent that they are unusable by anyone other than the legitimate owner unless a skilled technician is available to make alterations. Such a response becomes commercially feasible when a large organisation (local authority, hospital, commercial organisation) is purchasing, say, micro-computers, in bulk; it becomes sensible as a crime prevention measure, when it is widely known to be done.

Where homes are left empty for long and predictable periods of the day then traditional target hardening, simulated occupancy (achieved again through advances in technology) together with neighbourhood watch (perhaps making more systematic use of local, largely housebound old people) can reduce the risk of crime by making it more difficult to commit, increasing the degree of uncertainty in the offender's mind regarding his vulnerability and increasing, through surveillance, the risk of detection.

The development of crime prevention
Crime prevention has reached a critical point. The research activity of the late 70s and early 80s in England, Canada and Sweden; the preliminary indications of success of some local projects, and a concern about the growth in recorded crime have led to a substantial round of activity. But the position of crime prevention in central government policy has yet to be firmly established. In Canada, for example, Brantingham reports a move away from situational prevention and a growing interest in social measures, many of which have little or no obvious bearing on crime prevention. A similar ebb and flow of interest and emphasis can be seen in other countries. The work presented in this volume suggests that while prevention offers a valuable response to crime, it will require a sustained effort, at national and local level, if the difficulties (principally associated with stimulating public commitment and implementing preventive measures), are to be overcome. In short there is a need for a programme of work to carry forward what is at present a promising initiative. This programme will need to encompass research, publicity and local action.

Research
Further research and development work is vital if cost-effective measures of crime prevention are to be devised. Present policy and practice will soon have outgrown the ideas derived from previous research; new questions are constantly arising. Further research is necessary, to find out, for example, whether:

it is possible to predict the occurrence of displacement following preventive intervention; this suggests the need to develop the analysis of crime to encompass socio-demographic information and to devise ways of predicting, from analysis, changes in local patterns of crime;

situational prevention is, as Cornish and Clarke suggest, of value in tackling crimes which may have little geographical or temporal stability, for example, crimes of violence, sexual crime or racial attacks;

it is possible to identify why some people are prepared to undertake preventive measures and others show little or no interest in protecting themselves or their property. This work, related to work on the cost of crime and the savings that might be made from preventive action, is essential if the community, including its representatives from industry and commerce, are to be persuaded to contribute fully to preventive action, and

more research is also needed to clarify the ideas underlying social prevention. There is a tradition of criminological research – dating back to the original work of the Chicago school – which suggests the relevance of social organisations and neighbourhood experience to criminal behaviour. We need to re-examine research in this tradition and to set in hand fresh empirical studies if we are to offer advice on methods of social organisation in schools, neighbourhoods and housing estates which can reduce crime. Such a research programme is not discussed in this book which has concentrated on the practical developments remaining to be explored within situational crime prevention.

Publicity
The gap between research effort and practical action is substantial. It is territory where many good ideas go to waste. If it is to be bridged it is essential that members of the public come to recognise, and act on their recognition, that they can contribute directly to the reduction of crime and so enjoy a safer community. The difficulty of motivating the public to take preventive action is substantial. The prevention of crime does not hold the same place in the public's mind as, say the control of drugs, the reduction of traffic accidents, the reduction of accidents in the home or even energy conservation. The reason for this is obvious. While in aggregate terms the levels of crime in most western societies are high and rising, as far as the individual is concerned – apart from those trapped within the inner cities – the likelihood of becoming a victim of crime is comparatively low. Moreover, most have the insurance market to fall back on for support should they become the victim of crime.

The reduction of crime remains, therefore, essentially a task for somebody else, normally the police, and while the individual member of the public may acknowledge a collective benefit from preventive action, he is less likely to perceive a direct benefit to himself. There is a need therefore for promotional activity to change public attitudes and to do so in such a way that leads to acceptable preventive action against crime by the public. Such activity, which would have many parts (commercial advertising; dissemination of information through seminars and conferences and training programmes for key-occupational groups) must sell the simple message that preventive measures, taken by members of the public either as individuals or as representatives of groups, can actually reduce crime, and that as a result people and property are safer, and the community a better place in which to live. Promotional activity must create a climate within which prevention is seen to be the sensible and intelligent thing to do.

Much of this promotional activity will be aimed at the general public but where it is targetted, for example, at those departments and organisations providing services for the public sector, the task is to establish a belief that a satisfactory public service should meet not only traditional criteria (for example, adequate building, educational or medical standards etc.) but also contribute to the reduction in crime. Thus it is not sufficient to ensure that people are transported from A to B; it is also important (and part of the service) they they are not assualted on the way. Similarly, those attending the casualty wards of hospitals or local supplementary benefit offices should be able to do so without fear of being attacked.

Action at local level
The sustained development of prevention calls for action on the ground, locally orchestrated and carried through. It is not enough for the criminologists to research the area or for the publicist to give voice to the results of their work. Effort must be directed at creating situations within which practitioners can put ideas to work. Schemes, projects and initiatives need to be established across the country, each carried forward at local level, in such a way as to channel local expertise in the most effective way to cope with the specific problems the community is facing.

There is no single organisation to which one might turn to promote these activities. It is of course tempting to suggest that the police might be appropriate, with their organisational structure offering access from headquarters to beat level. But here administrative convenience is a criteria of only limited importance. And in any case, in the most crime ridden areas of the inner cities the police may be as unwelcome as the offender. The answer lies in encouraging other local agencies to take crime prevention within their mainstream activities where it must carry equal if not greater weight. Thus within England and Wales there is scope for working through regional industrial organisations, local chambers of trade and commerce, voluntary organisations, social services or local authorities. The community also offers a rich network of associations and organisations of different sizes, strengths and capabilities. Some have resources (for example within the industrial and commercial sectors); some have particular skills (builders, planners, designers) or particular insight into local community dynamics (the outreach youth worker); the task is to tap into these organisations and so promote prevention action. The diversity of schemes will be prodigious – indeed it is in this diversity and the close matching of local skills, preventive measures, and problems that gives strength to the approach.

The overall programme can be seen as a cycle of crime prevention action. The findings of research have already strengthened central government activity, particularly in stimulating local awareness. It is essential that the cycle is kept going, each activity feeding from and into the next, if the preventive response to crime is to be effective.

References

ABT Associates. (1980). *Midwood Kings Highway Development Corporation, Brooklyn, NY-Exemplary Project Validation Report.* Washington DC: US National.

Allatt, P. (1984). 'Residential security: containment and displacement of burglary'. *Howard Journal, 23,* 99-116.

Allatt, P. (1984). 'Fear of crime: the effect of improved residential security on a difficult to let estate'. *Howard Journal, 24* 170-182.

Angel, S. (1968). *Discouraging Crime Through City Planning* Working Paper No. 75, University of California, Institute of Urban and Regional Development, Berkeley.

Athens, L. (1980). *Violent Criminal Acts and Actors: A Symbolic Interactionist Study.* London: Routledge and Kegan Paul.

Baldwin, J. and Bottoms, A.E. (1976). *The Urban Criminal.* London: Tavistock Publications.

Barker, R.G. and Gump, P.V. (1964). *Big School, Small School.* Stanford, California: Stanford University Press.

Bayley, D.H. (1980). "Ironies of American Law Enforcement". *The Public Interest, 55,* 45-56.

Becker, G.S. (1968) "Crime and Punishment: An Economic Approach". *Journal of Polictical Economy, 76,* 169-217.

Bennett, T.W. and Wright, R. (1984). 'The relationship between alcohol use and burglary'. *British Journal of Addictions, 79,* 431-437.

Bennett, T.W. and Wright, R. (1984). *Burglars on Burglary: prevention and the offender.* Farnborough: Gower.

Beyleveld, D. (1982). "Ehrlich's analysis of deterrence". *British Journal of Criminology, 22,* 101-123.

Box, S. (1981). *Deviance, Reality and Society.* London: Holt, Rinehart and Winston.

Brantingham, P.L. and Brantingham, P.J. (1984). *Patterns in Crime.* New York: Macmillan Publishing Company. (Printed in London by Collier Macmillan Publishers).

Brantingham, P.J., Brantingham P.L. and Fister, R. (1979). "Mental Maps of Crime in Canadian City". *Paper presented at the Academy of Criminal Justice Sciences,* Cincinnati, Ohio.

Brantingham, P.J. and Faust, F.L. (1976). "A conceptual Model of Crime Prevention". *Crime and Delinquency, 22,* 284-296.

Briar, S. and Piliavin, I. (1965). "Delinquency, Situational Inducements and Commitment to Conformity". *Social Problems, 13,* 33-45.

Bright, J. and Petterson, G. (1984). *The Safe Neighbourhoods Unit.* London: NACRO.

Burgess, E., Lohman, J. and Shaw, C. (1937). "The Chicago Area Project". *National Probation Association Yearbook.*

Burrows, J. (1980). "Closed circuit television and crime on the London Underground". In: Clarke, R.V.G. and Mayhew, P (Eds) *Designing Out Crime.* London: HMSO.

Burrows, J. (1986). "Burglary: Police actions and victims views". *Home Office Research and Planning Unit Paper,* No. 37. London: HMSO.

Burrows, J. and Tarling R. (1982). *Clearing up Crime.* Home Office Research Study No. 73. London: HMSO.

Canada-British Columbia Travel Industry Development Subsidiary Agreement (TIDSA). (1983). *Port Alberni Harbourfront: Feasibility* Canada and British Columbia Joint Publication.

Canadian Association of Chiefs of Police, Crime Prevention Committee. (1975). *Crime Prevention Programmes: Canadian Police Departments.*

Carroll, J.S. (1978). "A Psychological Approach to Deterrence: The Evaluation of Criminal Opportunities". *Journal of Personality and Social Psychology, 36,* 1512-1520.

Chaiken, J.M., Lawless, M.W. and Stevenson, K.A. (1974). *Impact of Police Activity on Crime: Robberies on the New York City Subway System.* Report No. R-1424-N.Y.C. Santa Monica, California: Rand Corporation.

Cicourel, A. (1968). *The Social Organisation of Juvenile Justice* New York: Wiley.

Cirel, P., Evans, P., McGillis, D. and Whitcomb, D. (1977). *Community Crime Prevention, Seattle, Washington: An Exemplary Project.* Washington: Government Printing Office.

Citizen's Report. (1984). "Crime on the Block". Citizen's Report, *8,* No. 2.

Clarke, R.V.G. (1980). 'Situational crime prevention: theory and practice'. *British Journal of Criminology, 20,* 136-145.

Clarke, R. (1981). "The Prospects for Controlling Crime". *Home Office Research Bulletin, 12,* 12-19.

Clarke, R.V.G. (1983). "Situational Crime Prevention". In Tonry, M. and Morris, N. (Eds.) *Crime and Justice: an Annual review of research 4.* Chicago: University of Chicago Press.

Clarke, R.V. and Cornish, D.B. (1983). *Crime Control in Britain: A Review of Policy Research.* Albany: State University of New York Press.

Clarke, R.V. and Cornish, D.B. (1985). "Modeling Offenders' Decisions: a framework for policy and research" In, Tonry, M. and Morris, N. (Eds.) *Crime and Justice: an annual review of research 6.* Chicago: University of Chicago Press.

Clarke, R.V. and Hope, T. (1984). *Coping With Burglary: Research Perspectives on Policy.* Boston: Kluwer-Nijhoff.

Clarke, R.V.G. and Hough, M. (1984). *Crime and Police Effectiveness.* Home Office Research Study No. 79. London: HMSO.

Clarke, R.V.G. and Mayhew, P. (Eds.). (1980). *Designing out Crime.* London: HMSO.

Cloward, R. A. and Ohlin, L. (1960). *Delinquency and Opportunity.* Chicago: Free Press.

Cohen, A. K. (1956). *Delinquent Boys: The Culture of the Gang.* London: Routledge and Kegan Paul.

Conklin, J. E. (1981). *Criminology.* New York: MacMillan.

Cook, P. J. (1980). "Criminal deterrence: laying the goundwork for the second decade". In Tonry, M. and Morris, N. (Eds.) *Crime and Justice: an annual review of research. 2.* Chicago: University of Chicago Press.

Cornish, D. (1978). *Gambling: A Review of the Literature and its Implications for Policy and Research.* Home Office Research Study, No. 42, London: HMSO.

Crenson, M. (1983). Neighbourhood Politics. Cambridge MA: Harvard University Press

Crime Prevention News. (1982). Issue No. 3. London: HMSO.

Crime Prevention News. (1984). Issue No. 2. London: HMSO.

Crust, P. E. (1975). *Criminal Investigation Project.* Home Office Research Services Unit (unpublished).

Decker, J. F. (1972). 'Curbside deterrence: an analysis of the effects of a slug-rejector device, coin view window and warning labels on slug usage in New York City parking meters'. *Criminolgy,* August. 127-142.

Department of Education and Science/Welsh Office (1977). *A Study of School Building* Report by an Inter-Departmental Group. London: HMSO.

137

Department of Scientific and Industrial Research. (1962). *Road Research 1961.* London: HMSO.

Dobash, R. and Dobash, R. P. (1984). "The Nature and Antecedents of Violent Events". *British Journal of Criminology, 24,* 269-288.

Dollard, J., Miller, N. E., Doob, L. W. , Mowrer, O. H. and Sears, R. R. (1944). *Frustration and Aggression.* London: Kegan Paul, Trench, Trubner and Co., Ltd.

Duncan, J. T. S. (1980). *Citizen Crime Prevention Tactics: A Literature Review and Selected Bibliography.* NCJRS. Washington: Government Printing Office.

Eck, J. (1983). "Solving Crimes". Washington DC: National Institute of Justice.

Edwards, W. (1954). "The Theory of Decision Making". *Psychological Bulletin, 51,* 380-417.

Ehrlich, I. (1975). "The deterrent effect of capital punishment". *American Economic Review, 65,* 397-417.

Ehrlich, I. (1982). "On positive methodology, ethics and polemics in deterrence research". *British Journal of Criminology, 22,* 124-139.

Ekblom, P. J. (1986). "The prevention of shop theft: an approach through crime analysis". Home Office Crime Prevention Unit Paper No. 5. London: HMSO.

Engstad, P. and Evans, J. L. (1980). 'Responsibility, competence and police effectiveness in crime control'. In, Clarke, R. V. G. and Hough, J. M. (Eds.), *The Effectiveness of Policing.* Farnborough: Gower.

Erez, E. (1979). *Situational Analysis of Crime: Comparison of planned and impulsive offences.* PhD. dissertation, London: University Microfilms International.

Farrington, D. P. and Dowds, E. A. (1985). 'Disentangling criminal behaviour and police reaction'. In, Farrington, D. P. and Gunn, J. (Eds.), *Reaction to Crime: the public, the police, courts, and prisons.* Chichester: John Wiley.

Ferri, E. (1895). *Criminal Sociology* London: Fisher Unwin.

Fowler, F. J., McCalla, M. E. and Mangione, T. W. (1982). *Reducing Residential Crime and Fear: The Hartford Neighbourhood Crime Prevention Program.* U.S. Department of Justice, Washington: Government Printing Office.

Freud, S. (1940) "An Outline of Psycho-analysis". In, Strachey, J. (Ed.) (1955). Standard edition of the complete works of Sigmund Freud, *23,* 144-207. London: Hogarth Press.

Gabor, T. (1978). "Crime Displacement: The Literature and Strategies for Its Investigation". *Crime and Justice, 6,* 100-106.

Gardiner, R. A. (1978). *Design for Safe Neighbourhoods.* Washington, DC: Government Printing Office.

Gibbons, D. (1981). "Observations on the Study of Crime Causation". *American Journal of Sociology, 77,* 262-278.

Gibbs, J. J. and Shelly, P. L. (1982). "Life in the Fast Lane: A Retrospective View by Commercial Thieves". *Journal of Research in Crime and Delinquency, 19,* 299-330.

Gladstone, F. J. (1980). *Co-ordinating Crime Prevention Efforts.* Home Office Research Study, No. 62, London: HMSO.

Goldstein, H. (1977). "Policing a Free Society". Cambridge MA: Ballinger.

Greater London Council/Inner London Education Authority. (1977). "Designing for Security in Educational Buildings". In, *Schools Design Guide.* Department of Architecture and Civic Design.

Greenberg, D. F. (1977). 'Delinquency and the age structure of society'. *Contemporary Crises, 1,* 189-223.

Greenberg, S. W., Rohe, W. M. and Williams, J. R. (1984). "Informal Citizen Action and Crime Prevention at the Neighbourhood Level". Volumes I-IV. Research Triangle Park, N. Carolin: Research Triangle Institute.

Greenwood, P. W. (1984). "Selective incapacitation: a method of using our prisons more effectively". *Selective Notification of Information No. 183.* Washington DC: National Institute of Justice.

Greenwood, P. W., Petersilia, J. and Zimring, F. E. (1980). *Age, crime, and sanction: the transition from juvenile to adult court.* Santa Monica: Rand Corporation.

Guardian, The. (1983). January 3rd.

Hackler, J. (1978). *The Prevention of Youthful Crime: The Great Stumble Forward.* Toronto: Methuen.

Hakim, S. and Rengert, G. F. (1981). *Crime Spillover.* Beverly Hills: Sage.

Hampshire Constabulary. (1985). *Incident Pattern Analysis.* Hampshire Constabulary.

Healey, W. and Bronner, A. (1936). *New Light on Delinquency and Its Treatment.* New Haven, Connecticut: Yale University Press.

Hedges, A., Blaber, A. and Mostyn, B. (1980). *Community Planning Project: Cunningham Road Improvement Scheme.* London: Institute of Social and Community Planning Research.

Heller, M. B., Stenzel, W. W., Gill, A. D., Kolde, R. A. and Schimerman, S. R. (1975). *Operation Identification – An Assessment of Effectiveness.* National Evaluation Program – Phase 1 report. US Department of Justice, Washington DC: Government Printing Office.

Hest, J. J. and Harrison, J. T. J. (1983). *Policing the Port Alberni Habourfront Project*. Port Alberni, British Columbia: Crime Prevention Unit, Royal Canadian Mounted Police.

Hirschi, T. (1969). *Causes of Delinquency*. Berkeley and Los Angeles: University of California Press.

Hope, T. J. (1980). "Four approaches to the prevention of property crime in schools". *Oxford Review of Education, 6*, 231-240.

Hope, T. (1982). *Burglary in Schools: the prospects for prevention*. Research and Planning Unit Paper II. London: HMSO.

Hope, T. (1985). *Implementing Crime Prevention Measures*. Home Office Research Study No. 86. London: HMSO.

Hope, T. and Murphy, D. J. I. (1983). 'Problems of implementing crime prevention: the experience of a demonstration project'. *The Howard Journal of Penology and Crime Prevention*, XXII, 38-50.

Hotson, B. (1969). "Thefts from Prepayment Meters". (unpublished). Institute of Criminology, University of Cambridge.

Hough, J. M., Clarke, R. V. G., and Mayhew, P. (1980). 'Introduction'. In, Clarke, R. V. G. and Mayhew, P. (Eds.). *Designing out Crime. London: HMSO*.

Hough, M. and Mayhew, P. (Eds.) (1982). *Crime and Public Housing*, Research and Planning Unit Paper No. 6. London: Home Office Research and Planning Unit.

Hough, M. and Mayhew, P. (1983). *The British Crime Survey: first report*. Home Office Research Study No. 76. London: HMSO.

Humphreys, L. (1970). *"Tearoom Trade: Impersonal sex in public places"*. Chicago: Aldine.

Jacobs, J. (1961). *The Death and Life of Great American Cities*. New York: Random House. (Published by Penguin Books Ltd., Harmondsworth, in 1965).

Jeffery, C. R. (1971, 1977). *Crime Prevention Through Environmental Design*. Beverly Hills, CA: Sage.

Kelling, G. L. (1981). "Conclusions" in The Newark Foot Patrol Experiment. Washington D.C.: Police Foundation.

Knutsson, J. and Kuhlhorn, E. (1981). *Macro-Measures Against Crime*. Information Bulletin, No. 1. Stockholm:National Swedish Council for Crime Prevention.

Knuttson, J. (1984). *Operation Identification – a way to prevent burglaries?* National Council for Crime Prevention, Sweden, Report No. 14.

Kuschmuk, J. and Whittemore, S. L. (1981). *A Re-evaluation of Crime Prevention Through Environmental Design in Portland, Oregon.* Washington, DC: US National Institute of Justice.

Lavrakas, P. and Herg, E. (1982). "Citizen Participation in Neighbourhood Anti-Crime Measures" *Criminology, 20,* 479-498.

Laycock, G. (1985). *Property marking: a deterrent to domestic burglary?* Home Office Crime Prevention Unit Paper No 3. London: HMSO.

Laycock, G. (1984). *Reducing burglary: a study of chemists' shops.* Home Office Crime Prevention Unit Paper No 1. London: HMSO.

Lipsey, M. W. (1984). "Is Delinquency Prevention A Cost-Effective Strategy? A Californian Perspective". *Journal of Research in Crime and Delinquency. 21* No. 4.

Lombroso, C. (1911). *Crime, its Causes and Remedies.* London: Heinemann.

Lorenz, K. (1966). *On Aggression.* New York: Harcourt, Brace and Jovanovich.

Maguire, M. (1980). "Burglary As Opportunity". *Research Bulletin,* No. 10, London: Home Office Research Unit.

Maguire, M. in collaboration with Bennett, T. (1982) *Burglary in a Dwelling.* London: Heinemann.

Marsh, P., Rosser, E., and Harre, R. (1978), *The Rules of Disorder.* London: Routledge and Kegan Paul.

Mattick, H. W., Olander, C. K., Baker, D. G. and Schegel, H. E. (1974). *An evaluation of "operation identification" as operated in Illinois.* Center for Research in Criminal Justice, University of Illinois.

Matza, D. (1964). *Delinquency and Drift.* New York: Wiley.

Mawby, R. I. (1977). "Defensible Space: A Theoretical and Empirical Appraisal". *Urban Studies,* 14, 169-179.

Mayer, N. S. and Blake, J. L. (1980). "Keys to the Growth of Neighbourhood Development Organizations". Washington D.C.: The Urban Institute.

Mayhew, P. M., Clarke, R. V. G., Sturman, A. and Hough J. M. (1976). *Crime As Opportunity.* Home Office Research Study, No. 34. London: HMSO.

Mayhew, P., Clarke, R. V. G. and Hough, J. M. (1980). "Steering Column locks and car theft". In: Clarke, R. V. G. and Mayhew, P. (Eds.) *Designing Out Crime.* London: HMSO.

Mayhew, P. (1979). "Defensible Space: The Current Status of a Crime Prevention Theory". *The Howard Journal, XVIII,* 150-159.

Mayhew, P. (1984). "Target Hardening: How Much of an Answer?" In Clarke, R. V. G. and Hope, T. (Eds.), *Coping with Burglary,* Boston: Kluwer-Nijhoff.

McClintock, F. H. (1963). *Crimes of Violence.* London: Macmillan.

McInnes, P., Burgess, G., Hann, R. and Axon, L. (1962). *The Environmental Design and Management (EDM) Approach to Crime Prevention in Residential Environments. Canada: Report for the Research Division of the Department of the Solicitor General and The Technical Research Division, Policy Development and Research Sector of the Canadian Mortgage and Housing Corporation.*

McPherson, M. (1982). *The Future of Community Crime Prevention: a Retrospective Examination.* Minneapolis, Minn: Minnesota Crime Prevention Centre, Inc.

Mischel, W. (1968). *Personality and Assessment.* New York: Wiley

Moore, M. H. and Kelling, G. L. (1983). "To serve and Protect: Learning From Police History". *Public Interest, 70,* Winter: 49-65.

National Institute of Education (1978). *Violent Schools – Safe Schools the Safe School Study Report to Congress, 1.* Washington, DC: US Department of Health, Education and Welfare.

Newman, O. (1973). *Defensible Space.* London: Architecture Press.

Nisbett, R. and Ross, L. (1980). *Human Inference: Strategies and Shortcomings of Social Judgement.* Englewood Cliffs, New Jersey: Prentice-Hall.

Normandeau, A. and Hasenpusch, B. (1978). *Review of Active Crime Prevention Methods: Vol 2.* Montreal: Ecole de Criminologie, Universite de Montreal.

Ohlin, L. (1971). "A Situational Approach to Delinquency Prevention". Washington D.C.: Department of Health, Education and Welfare.

Olson, M. R. (1972). 'A longitudinal analysis of official criminal careers'. Doctoral dissertation, University of Iowa, Iowa City.

Parker, H. J. (1974). *View From the Boys: A Sociology of Down-Town Adolescents.* Newton Abbot: David and Charles.

Pate, T., Bowers, R. A. and Parks R. (1976). "Three Approaches to Criminal Apprehension". Washington DC.: Police Foundation.

Payne, J. (1980). "Information Processing Theory: Some Concepts and Methods Applied to Decision Research". In: Wallston, T. (Ed.), *Cognitive Processes in Choice and Decision Behaviour,* Hillside, New Jersey: Erlbaum.

Petersilia, J. (1980) "Criminal career research". In Tonry, M. and Morris, N. (Eds.) *Crime and justice: an annual review of research. 2.* Chicago: University of Chicago Press.

Petersilia, J., Greenwood, P. W., and Lavin, M. (1978). *"Criminal careers of convicted felons".* Washington, DC: U.S. Government Printing Office.

Petersilia, J. and Greenwood, P. W. (1978). "Mandatory prison sentences: their projected effects on crime and prison populations". *Journal of Criminal Law and Criminology, 69,* 604-15.

Peterson, N. A. and Braiker, H. B. with Polich, S. M. (1980). *Doing crime: a survey of Calfornian prison inmates.* Santa Monica: Rand Corporation.

Podolefsky, A. (1983). *Case studies in Community Crime Prevention.* Springfield, III: Charles C. Thomas.

Police Foundation (1981). "The Newark Foot Patrol Experiment". Washington DC: Police Foundation.

Poyner, B. (1980). *Personal Factors in Domestic Accidents: Prevention through Product and Environmental Design.* London: Department of Trade.

Poyner, B. (1980b). *A Study of Street Attacks and their Environmental Settings.* London: The Tavistock Institute of Human Relations.

Poyner, B. (1981). "Crime prevention and the environment" *Police Research Bulletin,* No. 37, 10-18.

Poyner, B. (1983). *Design Against Crime.* London: Butterworths.

Quinney, R. (1970). The Social Reality of Crime, Boston: Brown.

Ramsay, M. N. (1982). *City-Centre Crime: the scope for situational prevention.* Research and Planning Unit Paper 10. London: Home Office.

Ramsay, M. N. and Heal, K. H. (1982)."Crime analysis: an approach to crime prevention". *Police Research Bulletin.* No. 38, 23-37.

Rengert, G. F. and Wasilchick, J. In press. *Suburban Burglary: A Time and a Place for Everything.* Springfield, Illinois: Charles C. Thomas.

Reppetto, T. A. (1974). *Residential Crime.* Cambridge, Massachusettes: Ballinger.

Reppetto, T. A. (1976). "Crime Prevention and the Displacement Phenomenon" *Crime and Delinquency, 22,* 166-177.

Reppetto, T. A. (1984). "Police Anti-Burglary Strategies in the United States" In Clarke, R. V. and Hope, T. (Eds.) *Coping with Burglary.* Boston: Kluwger-Nijhoff.

Reynolds, D. and Jones, D. (1978). "Education and the prevention of juvenile delinquency", in Tutt N. (Ed.) *Alternative Strategies for Coping with Crime.* Oxford: Blackwell.

Rich, R. C. (1980). "The Dynamics of Leadership in Neighbourhood Organizations". *Social Science Quarterly, 60,* 570-587.

143

Ross, B. H. (1979). "Improving the Management of Neighbourhood Organisations". *South Atlantic Studies, 4,* 32-41.

Rowe, W. E. (1981). *The Evaluation of "Operational" Social Services Programs: Major Issues and Implications for Juvenile Delinquency Prevention Programs.* British Columbia: Ministry of the Attorney General.

Rowe, W. E. and Edelman, S. (1982). *A Systems Evaluation of Burnaby Youth Services: A Police Based Youth and Family Councelling Program.* British Columbia: Ministry of the Attorney General.

Rutter, M., Maughan, B., Mortimore, P., and Ouston, J. (1979). *Fifteen Thousand Hours: Secondary Schools and their effects on children.* London: Open Books.

Rutter, M. and Giller, H. (1983). *Juvenile Delinquency: Trends and Perspectives.* Harmondsworth, Middlesex: Penguin Books.

Sagalin, A. and others (1973). Residential security. Washington, D.C.: National Institute of Law Enforcement and Criminal Justice.

Schwartz, B. (1968). "The effects in Philadelphia of Pennsylvania's increased penalties for rape and attempted rape". *Journal of Criminal Law, Criminology and Police Science, 59,* 509-515.

Seaborne, M. and Lowe, M. (1977). *The English School, Its Architecture and Organisation, 2, 1870-1970.* London: Routledge and Kegan Paul.

Sellin, T. (1980). *The penalty of death.* Beverly Hills: Sage.

Shannon, L. W. (1978). "A longitudinal study of delinquency and crime". In C. Wellford (Ed.) *Quantitative studies in criminology* Beverly Hills: Sage.

Shaw, C. R. and Mackay, H. D. (1969). *Juvenile Delinquency and Urban Area,* (Rev. Ed.) Chicago: University of Chicago Press.

Southall, D. and Ekblom, P. J. (1985). *Designing for vehicle security: towards a crime free car.* Home Office Crime Prevention Unit Paper No. 5. London: HMSO.

Sturman, A. (1978). "Measuring Vandalism in a city surburb". In Clarke, R. V. G. (Ed.) *Tackling Vandalism.* Home Office Research Study No. 47. London: HMSO.

Sturman, A. (1980). "Damage on buses: The effects of supervision". In Clarke, R. V. G. and Mayhew, P. (Eds.), *Designing Out Crime.* London: HMSO.

Sutherland, E. and Cressey, D. (1955). *Criminology.* Philadelphia: Lippincott.

Skogan, W. G. and Antunnes, G. E. (1979). "Information, Apprehension and Deterrence: Exploring the Limits of Police Productivity". *Journal of Criminal Justice, 7:3.*

Titus, R. M. (1982). "Citizen and Environmental Crime Prevention". Washington DC: National Institute of Justice.

Trasler, G. B. (1978). "Psychopathy and persistent criminality – theoretical and methodological issues". In Hare, R. D. and Schalling, D. (Eds.) *Psychopathic behaviour: approaches to research.* New York: Wiley.

Trasler, G. B. (1979). "Vandalism". *British Journal of Crimonology, 19,* 168-170.

Trasler, G. B. (1979). "Delinquency, Recidivism, and Desistance". *British Journal of Criminology, 19,* 314-322.

Trojanowicz, R. C. (1983). "The Neighbourhood Foot Patrol Program". East Lansing, MI: Michigan State University.

Trojanowicz, R. C. and Banas, D. W. (1985,a). "Job satisfaction: A Comparison of Foot Patrol Versus Motor Patrol Officers". East Lansing, MI: Michigan State University.

Trojanwicz, R. C. and Banas, D. W. (1985,b). "Perceptions of Safety". East Lansing, MI: Michigan State University.

von Hirsch, A. (1984). *Selective incapacitation: a method of using our prisons more effectively.* Selective notification of Information No. 185. Washington, DC: National Institute of Justice.

Waller, I. (1979). "What Reduces Residential Burglary: Action and Research in Seattle and Toronto". Paper presented at the Third International Symposium on Victimology, Muenster, West Germany.

Waller, I. and Okihiro, T. (1978). *Burglary: The Victim and the Public.* Toronto: University of Toronto Press.

Walsh, P. (1978). *Shoplifting: Controlling a Major Crime.* London: Macmillan.

Walsh, P. (1980). *Break-Ins: Burglary from Private Houses.* London: Constable.

Warren, R. B. and Warren, D. I. (1977). "The Neighbourhood Organizers Handbook". Notre Dame, Indiana: Notre Dame Press.

West, D. J. (1963). *The Habitual Prisoner.* London: Macmillan.

West, D. J. (1982). *Delinquency: Its Roots, Careers and Prospects.* London: Heinemann.

West, D. J. (1983). "Sex offenses and offending". In Tonry, M. and Morris, N. (Eds.) *Crime and Justice: an annual review of research 5.* Chicago: University of Chicago Press.

West, D. J., Roy, C. and Nichols, F. L. (1978). *Understanding sexual attacks.* London: Heinmann.

West, W. G. (1978). "The Short Term Careers of Serious Thieves". *Canadian Journal of Criminology, 20,* 169-190.

Wilkinson, P. (1977). *Terrorism and the Liberal State.* London: Macmillan.

Wilson, S. (1980). "Vandalism and defensible space on London housing estates". In, Clarke, R. V. G. and Mayhew, P. (Eds.), *Designing Out Crime.* London: HMSO.

Wilson, J. Q. and Kelling, G. L. (1982). "The Police and Neighbourhood Safety". *Atlantic,* March, 29-38.

Winchester, S. and Jackson, H. (1982). *Residential Burglary: The Limits of Prevention.* Home Office Research Study, No. 74. London: HMSO.

Witte, A. D., Tauchen, H. V. and Long, S. K. (1984). *Violence in the Family: A Non-Random Affair.* Working Paper No. 89, Department of Economics, Wellesley College.

Wood, E. (1961). *Housing Design: A Social Theory.* New York: Citizens' Housing and Planning Council.

Worrell, P. B. (1984). *An Evaluation of the Neighbourhood Watch Program in Thunder Bay.* Ottawa: Ministry of the Solicitor General.

Yin, R. K. (1982). "Conserving America's Neighbourhoods". New York: Plenum Press.

Zeisel, J. (1976). *Stopping School Property Damage: design and administrative guidelines to reduce school vandalism.* Arlington, Virginia: American Association of School Administrators.

Subject Index

147

Telephone kiosks 21
Television 87
Terraced property 56
Territoriality 45, 46, 50
Theft from the person, see also Robbery 118
Theories of crime see also, Models of crime: 21
  choice 4, 15*ff*, 41, 43, 124
  deterministic 5, 22
  dispositional 17, 43
  drive 2, 4, 6*ff*
  economic 5*ff*, 19*ff*, 103
  strain 3
Tokens 5, 111
Tourism 109
Town centres 111
Traffic 109
Traffic flow 52
Training 104, 107, 114, 121
Transport 35, 82, 120
Treatment 21, 41, 104
Trethomas 59*ff*
Trouble spots 81

Ultra-violet pens, see Marking equipment
Underpasses 17
United Kingdom 19, 43, 55, 57, 69, 123
United States 43, 56, 68, 69
Unoccupied buildings 45
Unprotected homes 56

Urban budgetting 100
Urban decay 17*ff*
Urban unrest 101
Utilitarian 20, 23

Vandalism 17, 22, 79, 84, 110, 127
Verbal stimuli 46
Victim's survey 62
Victimisation 22, 28, 33*ff*, 56*ff*, 87, 106
Video games 111
Vigilante-ism 100, 101, 106
Voluntary organisations 93, 94, 123, 125
Volunteers 106, 112

Wages 19
Waterfront 109
Weapons 95
Welfare: 103*ff*
  criminality 113*ff*
West Germany 2
West Island, Montreal 112
Wife battering 6, 127
Window decals 56*ff*, 63*ff*, 105
Window locks 46
Working conditions 114
Wounding 32, 82

Youth centres 77
Youths, see Juvenile

Author Index

154

Southall, D. 127, 129
Stenzel, W.W. See, Heller, M.B.
Stevenson, K.A. See, Chaiken, J.M.
Sturman, A. 127
Sturman, A. See, Mayhew, P.
Sutherland, E. 43

Tarling, R. See, Burrows, J.
Tauchen, H.V. See, Witte, A.D.
Titus, R.M. 91
Trasler, G.B. 14, 20, 127
Trojanowicz, R.C. 97, 100, 101

Waller, I. 42, 52
Walsh, P. 12, 22, 52
Warren, D.I. See, Warren, R.B.
Warren, R.B. 96
Wasilchick, J. See, Rengert, G.F.
West, D.J. 14, 15, 20

West, W.G. 14
Whitcomb, D. See, Cirel, P.
Whittemore, S.L. See, Kuschmuk, J.
Wilkinson, P. 1
Williams, J.R. See, Greenberg, S.W.
Wilson, J.Q. 100, 101
Wilson, S. 127
Winchester, S. 11, 52, 127
Witte, A.D. 6
Wood, E. 43
Worrell, P.B. 107
Wright, R. See, Bennett, T.W.

Yates 100
Yin, R.K. 96, 97

Zeisel, J. 77
Zimring, F.E. See, Greenwood, P.W.

Notes on Contributors

TREVOR BENNETT is a Senior Research Associate at the Institute of Criminology, University of Cambridge. He has been responsible for a number of Home Office funded research projects including studies of the perceptions of convicted burglars, the attitudes and behaviour of heroin and methadone addicts and, currently, an evaluation of neighbourhood watch schemes in London. Trevor Bennett's research on convicted burglars has recently been published as a book under the title "Burglars on Burglary".

PATRICIA BRANTINGHAM is an Associate Professor of Criminology at Simon Fraser University in British Colombia, Canada. She is currently Director of Programme Evaluation at the Department of Justice. Patricia Brantingham is a mathematician and urban planner by training and much of her work is in environmental criminology and urban planning approaches in crime prevention. Her recent publications include "Environmental Criminology" and "Patterns of Crime".

RONALD CLARKE is Professor of Criminal Justice at Temple University, Philadelphia, and was previously Head of the Home Office Research and Planning Unit, London. During his time at the Home Office he undertook studies of residential treatment for delinquents, and played a major role in the development of both situational crime prevention and the British Crime Survey. He is the author of several papers and monographs, and joint editor of several books on the effectiveness of policing, issues in crime prevention and criminal decision making. He trained as a clinical psychologist and obtained his PhD from London University in 1968.

DEREK CORNISH, after working in the Home Office Research Unit for a number of years, joined the Department of Social Science Administration at the London School of Economics, where he teaches psychology, social research and criminology. In addition to his own research on gambling, he has co-authored a number of books, reports and articles on criminological topics with Ronald Clarke. His current research interests are: the history of assessment; evaluating institutional treatment for delinquents; criminal decision making, and gambling.

KEVIN HEAL, having begun his career with the British Meteorological Service, studied at the London School of Economics and subsequently joined the Department of Sociology, University of Essex. On joining the Home Office Research and Planning Unit in 1971 he carried out research on the impact of community homes and schools on children's behaviour and was subsequently responsible for establishing a programme of research on the police within the Home Office. In 1983 he was appointed Head of the then newly formed Home Office Crime Prevention Unit.

In that year he was also appointed consultant to the Council of Europe Select Committee of Experts on Crime Prevention.

TIM HOPE is a Senior Research Officer at the Home Office Research and Planning Unit. Trained as a sociologist, he joined the Home Office in 1974. He has published mainly in the field of crime prevention and environmental criminology. His research includes studies of school design and burglary, the implementation of preventive measures, vandalism in schools, disorder associated with licensed premises, neighbourhood watch, and community crime prevention. He is the joint editor of "Coping with Burglary".

GEORGE KELLING is a professor in the College of Criminal Justice at Northeastern University and a fellow in the Program in Criminal Justice Policy and Management in the Kennedy School of Government at Harvard University. His major works include co-authoring the Kansas City Preventive Patrol Experiment and the Newark Foot Patrol Experiment. His article in *The Atlantic* magazine with James Q. Wilson, "Broken Windows", has had a major impact on police and community crime control efforts in neighbourhoods in the United States.

GLORIA LAYCOCK joined the Prison Service as a psychologist in 1968 and was based for the following 10 years in Wormwood Scrubs prison. In 1978 she transferred to the Home Office Research and Planning Unit where she continued to carry out research on the prison system and on police cautioning policy. Since 1983 she has worked in the Home Office Crime Prevention Unit where, as Principal Research Officer, she is responsible for the research programme.

BARRY POYNER currently directs a programme of crime prevention research at the Tavistock Institute of Human Relations, London. He has worked in research groups at the War Office and the Ministry of Public Buildings and Works, and held a two year research fellowship at Birmingham School of Architecture before joining Scientific Control Systems Ltd, as a consultant in 1969. He joined the Tavistock Institute in 1971. Before coming involved in crime prevention research he was responsible for a programme of accident research.

MALCOLM RAMSAY is a Senior Research Officer, Home Office Research and Planning Unit. His publications cover aspects of homicide, crimes committed by women, muggings, hostels for ex-offenders, the use of imprisonment, and attitudes towards crime. He obtained his PhD from Edinburgh University for work on the development of imprisonment.

BO SVENSSON was born in Gotenborg, April 1940. He studied law in Lund and graduated in 1963. In 1979 Bo Svensson was appointed Director General of the National Swedish Council for Crime Prevention (NCCP). He is chairman of the Bureau of the European Committee on Crime Problems (CDPC), and of an expert committee on the Organisation of Crime Prevention set up by the Council of Europe. As a member of the United Nations Committee on Crime Prevention and Control, and Chairman of the Advisory Board of the Helsinki Institute affiliated with the United Nations (HEUNI), he also plays an active role in UN activities in the field of crime prevention.

GORDON TRASLER is Professor of Psychology in the University of Southampton, and has taught at the Institute of Criminology, University of Cambridge, the London School of Economics, and the University of Alberta at Edmonton. He was formerly a psychologist at Wandsworth and Winchester prisons. He was a member of the Younger Committee on Young Adult Offenders and the Wootton Committee on Non-custodial and Semi-custodial Penalties, and is an advisor to the Home Office on the evaluation of 'tougher' detention centres. He was Editor of the British Journal of Criminology from 1981 to 1985. He is a magistrate and the author of several books and many articles on crime and delinquency, and particularly the psychophysiology of criminality.

Publications

Titles already published for the Home Office

Studies in the Causes of Delinquency and the Treatment of Offenders (SCDTO)

1. Prediction methods in relation to borstal training. Hermann Mannheim and Leslie T. Wilkins, 1955 viii + 276pp. (11 340051 9).

2. *Time spend awaiting trial. Evelyn Gibson. 1960. v + 45pp. (34-368-2).

3. Delinquent generations. Leslie T. Wilkins. 1960. iv. + 20pp. (11 340053 5).

4. *Murder. Evelyn Gibson and S. Klein. 1961. iv + 44pp. (11 340054 3).

5. Persistent criminals. A study of all offenders liable to preventive detention in 1956. W. H. Hammond and Edna Chayen. 1963. ix + 237pp. (34-368-5).

6. *Some statistical and other numerical techniques for classifying individuals. P. McNaughton-Smith. 1965. v + 33pp. (34-368-6).

7. Probation research: a preliminary report. Part I. General outline of research. Part II. Study of Middlesex probation area (SOMPA). Steven Folkard, Kate Lyon, Margaret M. Carver and Erica O'Leary. 1966. vi + 58pp. (11 340374 7).

8. *Probation research: national study of probation. Trends and regional comparisons in probation (England and Wales). Hugh Barr and Erica O'Leary. 1966. vii + 51pp. (34-368-8).

9. *Probation research. A survey of group work in the probation service. Hugh Barr. 1966. vii + 94pp. (34-368-9).

10. *Types of delinquency and home background. A validation study of Hewitt and Jenkins' hypothesis. Elizabeth Field. 1967. vi + 21pp. (34-368-10).

11. *Studies of female offenders. No. 1 – Girls of 16-20 years sentenced to borstal or detention centre training in 1963. No. 2 – Women offenders in the Metroplitan Police District in March and April 1957. No. 3 – A description of women in prison on January 1, 1965. Nancy Goodman and Jean Price. 1967. v + 78pp. (34-368-11).

12. *The use of the Jesness Inventory on a sample of British probationers. Martin Davis. 1967 iv + 20pp. (34-368-12).

13. *The Jesness Inventory: application to approved school boys. Joy Mott. 1969. iv + 27pp. (11 340063 2).

Home Office Research Studies (HORS)

1. *Workloads in children's departments. Eleanor Grey. 1969. vi + 75pp. (11 340101 9).

2. *Probationers in their social environment. A study of male probationers aged 17-20, together with an analysis of those reconvicted within twelve months. Martin Davies. 1969. vii + 204pp. (11 340102 7).

3. *Murder 1957 to 1968. A Home Office Statistical Division report on murder in England and Wales. Evelyn Gibson and S. Klein (with annex by the Scottish Home and Health Department on murder in Scotland). 1969. vi + 94pp. (11 340103 5).

4. Firearms in crime. A Home Office Statistical Division report on indictable offences involving firearms in England and Wales. A. D. Weatherhead and B. M. Robinson. 1970. viii + 39pp. (11 340104 3).

5. *Financial penalties and probation. Martin Davis. 1970. vii + 39pp. (11 3240105 1).

*Out of print.

6. *Hostels for probationers. A study of the aims, working and variations in effectiveness of male probation hostels with special reference to the influence of the environment on delinquency. Ian Sinclair. 1971. ix + 200pp. (11 340106 X).

7. *Prediction methods in criminology – including a prediction study of young men on probation. Frances H. Simon. 1971. xi + 234pp. (11 340107 8).

8. *Study of the juvenile liaison scheme in West Ham 1961-65. Marilyn Tailor. 1971. vi + 46pp. (11 340108 6).

9. *Exploration in after-care. I – After-care units in London, Liverpool and Manchester. Martin Silberman (Royal London Prisoners' Aid Society) and Brenda Chapman. II – After-care hostels receiving a Home Office grant. Ian Sinclair and David Snow (HORU). III – St. Martin of Tours House, Ayreh Leissner (National Bureau for Co-operation in Child Care). 1971. xi + 140pp. (11 340109 4).

10. A survey of adoption in Great Britain. Eleanor Grey in collaboration with Ronald M. Blunden. 1971. ix + 168pp. (11 340110 8).

11. *Thirteen-year-old approved school boys in 1962. Elizabeth Field, W. H. Hammond and J. Tizard. 1971. ix + 46pp. (11 340111 6).

12. Absconding from approved schools. R. V. G. Clarke and D. N. Martin. 1971. vi + 146pp. (11 340112 4).

13. An experiment in personality assessment of young men remanded in custody. H. Sylvia Anthony. 1972. viii + 79pp. (11 340113 2).

14. *Girl offenders aged 17-20 years. I – Statistics relating to girl offenders aged 17-20 years from 1960 to 1970. II – Re-offending by girls released from borstal or detention centre training. III – The problems of girls released from borstal training during their period on after-care. Jean Davies and Nancy Goodman. 1972. v + 77pp. (11 340114 0).

15. *The controlled trial in institutional research – paradigm or pitfall for penal evaluators? R. V. G. Clarke and D. B. Cornish. 1972. v + 33pp. (11 340115 9).

16. *A survey of fine enforcement. Paul Softley. 1973. v+ 65pp. (11 340116 7).

17. *An index of social environment – designed for use in social work research. Martin Davies. 1973. vi + 63pp. (11 340117 5).

18. *Social enquiry reports and the probation service. Martin Davies and Andrea Knopf. 1973. v + 49pp. (11 340118 3).

19. *Depression, psychopathic personality and attempted suicide in a borstal sample. H. Sylvia Anthony. 1973. viii + 44pp. (0 11 340119 1).

20. *The use of bail and custody by London magistrates' courts before and after the Criminal Justice Act 1967. Frances Simon and Mollie Weatheritt. 1974. vi + 78pp. (0 11 340120 5).

21. *Social work in the environment. A study of one aspect of probation practice. Martin Davies, with Margaret Rayfield, Alaster Calder and Tony Fowles. 1974. ix + 151pp. (0 11 340121 3).

22. Social work in prison. An experiment in the use of extended contact with offenders. Margaret Shaw. vii + 154pp. (0 11 340122 1).

23. Delinquency amongst opiate users. Joy Mott and Marilyn Taylor. vi + 31pp. (01 340663 0).

24. IMPACT. Intensive matched probation and after-care treatment. Vol. I – The design of the probation experiment and an interim evaluation. M. S. Folkard, A. J. Fowles, B. C. McWilliams, W. McWilliams, D. D. Smith, D. E. Smith and G. R. Walmsley. 1974. v + 54pp. (0 11 340664 9).

25. The approved school experience. An account of boys' experiences of training under differing regimes of approved schools, with an attempt to evaluate the effectiveness of that training. Anne B. Dunlop. 1974, vii + 124pp. (0 11 340665 7).

26. *Absconding from open prisons. Charlotte Banks, Patricia Mayhew and R. J. Sapsford. 1975. viii + 89pp. (0 11 340666 5).

---

*Out of print

27. Driving while disqualified. Sue Kriefman. 1975. vi + 136pp. (0 11 340667 3).

28. Some male offenders' problems. I – Homeless offenders in Liverpool. W. McWilliams. II – Casework with short-term prisoners. Julie Holborn. 1975. x + 147pp. (011 340668 1).

29. *Community service orders. K. Pease, P. Durkin, I. Earnshaw, D. Payne and J. Thorpe. 1975. viii + 80pp. (0 11 340669 X).

30. Field Wing Bail Hostel: the first nine months. Frances Simon and Sheena Wilson. 1975. viii + 55pp. (0 11 340670 3).

31. Homicide in England and Wales 1967 - 1971. Evelyn Gibson. 1975. iv + 59pp. (0 11 340753 X).

32. Residential treatment and its effects on delinquency. D. B. Cornish and R. V. G. Clarke. 1975. vi + 74pp. (0 11 340672 X).

33. Further studies of female offenders. Part A: Borstal girls eight years after release. Nancy Goodman, Elizabeth Maloney and Jean Davies. Part B: The sentencing of women at the London Higher Courts. Nancy Goodman, Paul Durkin and Janet Halton. Part C: Girls appearing before a juvenile court. Jean Davies. 1976. vi + 114pp. (0 11 340673 8).

34. *Crime as opportunity. P. Mayhew, R. V. G. Clarke, A. Sturman and J. M. Hough. 1976. vii + 36pp. (0 11 340674 6).

35. The effectiveness of sentencing: a review of the literature. S. R. Brody. 1976. v + 89pp. (0 11 340675 4).

36. IMPACT. Intensive matched probation and after-care treatment. Vol. II – The results of the experiment. M. S. Folkard, D. E. Smith and D. D. 1976 xi + 400pp. (0 11 340676 2).

37. Police cautioning in England and Wales. J. A. Ditchfield. 1976. v + 31pp. (0 11 340677 2).

38. Parole in England and Wales. C. P. Nuttall, with E. E. Barnard, A. J. Fowles, A. Frost, W. H. Hammond, P. Mayhew, K. Pease, R. Tarling and M. J. Weatheritt. 1977. vi + 90pp. (0 11 340678 9).

39. Community service assessed in 1976. K. Pease, S. Billingham and I. Earnshaw. 1977. vi + 29pp. (0 11 340679 7).

40. Screen violence and film censorship: a review of research. Stephen Brody. 1977. vii + 179pp. (0 11 340680 0).

41. Absconding from borstals. Gloria K. Laycock. 1977. v + 82pp. (0 11 340681 9).

42. Gambling: a review of the literature and its implications for policy and research. D. B. Cornish. 1978. xii + 284pp. (0 11 340682 7).

43. Compensation orders in magistrates' courts. Paul Softley. 1978. v + 41pp. (0 11 340683 5).

44. Research in criminal justice. John Croft. 1978. iv + 16pp (0 11 340684 3).

45. Prison welfare: an account of an experiment at Liverpool. A. J. Fowles. 1978. v + 34pp. (0 11 340685 1).

46. Fines in magistrates' courts. Paul Softley. 1978. v + 42pp. (0 11 340686 X).

47. Tackling vandalism. R. V. G. Clarke (editor), F. J. Gladstone, A. Sturman and Sheena Wilson (contributors). 1978. vi + 91pp. (0 11 340687 8).

48. Social inquiry reports: a survey. Jennifer Thorpe. 1979. vi + 55pp. (0 11 340688 6).

49. Crime in public view. P. Mayhew, R. V. G. Clarke, J. N. Burrows, J. M. Hough and S. W. C. Winchester. 1979. v + 36pp. (0 11 340689 4).

50. *Crime and the community. John Croft. 1979. v + 16pp. (0 11 340690 8).

51. Life-sentence prisoners. David Smith (editor), Christopher Brown, Joan Worth, Roger Sapsford and Charlotte Banks (contributors). 1979. iv + 51pp. (0 11 340691 6).

52. Hostels for offenders. Jane E. Andrews, with an appendix by Bill Sheppard. 1979. v + 30pp. (0 11 340692 4).

---

*Out of print.

53. Previous convictions, sentence and reconviction: a statistical study of a sample of 5,000 offenders convicted in January 1971. G. J. O. Phillpotts and L. B. Lancucki. 1979. v + 55pp. (0 11 340693 2).

54. Sexual offences, consent and sentencing. Roy Walmsley and Karen White. 1979. vi + 77pp. (0 11 340694 0).

55. Crime Prevention and the police. John Burrows, Paul Ekblom and Kevin Heal. 1979. v + 37pp. (0 11 340695 9).

56. Sentencing practice in magistrates's courts. Roger Tarling, with the assistance of Mollie Weatheritt. 1979. vii + 54pp. (0 11 340696).

57. Crime and comparative research. John Croft. 1979. iv 16pp. (0 11 340697 5).

58. Race, crime and arrests. Philip Stevens and Carole F. Willis. 1979. v + 69pp. (0 11 3406983).

59. Research and criminal policy. John Croft. 1980. iv + 14pp. (0 11 340699 1).

60. Junior attendance centres. Anne B. Dunlop. 1980. v + 47pp. (0 11 340700 9).

61. Police interrogation: an observational study in four police stations. Paul Softley, with the assistance of David Brown, Bob Forde, George Mair and David Moxon. 1980. vii + 67pp. (0 11 340701 7).

62. Co-ordinating crime prevention efforts. F. J. Gladstone. 1980. v + 74pp. (0 11 340702 5).

63. Crime prevention publicity: an assessment. D. Riley and P. Mayhew. 1980. v + 47pp. (0 11 340703 3).

64. Taking offenders out of circulation. Stephen Brody and Roger Tarling. 1980. v + 46pp. (0 11 340704 1).

65. *Alcoholism and social policy: are we on the right lines? Mark Tuck. 1980. v + 30pp. (0 11 340705 X).

66. Persistent petty offenders. Suzan Fairhead. 1981. vi + 78pp. (0 11 340706 8).

67. Crime control and the police. Pauline Morris and Kevin Heal. 1981. v + 71pp. (0 11 340707 6).

68. Ethnic minorities in Britain: a study of trends in their positions since 1961. Simon Field, George Mair, Tom Rees and Philip Stevens. 1981. v + 48pp. (0 11 340708 4).

69. Managing criminological research. John Croft. 1981. iv + 17pp. (0 11 340709 2).

70. Ethnic minorities, crime and policing: a survey of the experiences of West Indians and whites. Mary Tuck and Peter Southgate. iv + 50pp. (0 11 32407653).

71. Contested trials in magistrates' courts. Julie Vennard. 1982. v + 32pp. (0 11 340766 1).

72. Public disorder: a review of research and a study in one inner city area. Simon Field and Peter Southgate. 1982. v + 77pp. (0 11 340767 X).

73. Clearing up crime. John Burrows and Roger Tarling. 1982. vii + 31pp. (0 11 340768 8).

74. Residential burglary: the limits of prevention. Stuart Winchester and Hilary Jackson. 1982. v + 47pp. (0 11 340769 6).

75. Concerning crime. John Croft. 1982. iv + 16pp. (0 11 340770 X).

76. The British Crime Survey: first report. Mike Hough and Pat Mayhew. 1983. v + 62pp. (0 11 340789 6).

77. Contact between police and public: findings from the British Crime Survey. Peter Southgate and Paul Ekblom. 1984. v + 42pp. (0 11 340771 8).

78. Fear of crime in England and Wales. Michael Maxfield. 1984. v + 51pp. (0 11 340772 6).

79. Crime and police effectiveness. Ronald V. Clarke and Mike Hough. 1984. iv + 33pp. (0 11 340773 4).

80. The attitudes of ethnic minorities. Simon Field. 1984. v + 50pp. (0 11 340774 2).

81. Victims of crime: the dimensions of risk. Michael Gottfredson. 1984. v + 54pp. (0 11 32407750).

---

*Out of print

82. The tape recording of police interviews with suspects: an interim report. Carole Willis. 1984. v + 45pp. (0 11 340776 9).

83. Parental supervision and juvenile delinquency. David Riley and Margaret Shaw. 1985. v + 90pp. (0 11 340799 8).

84. Adult prisons and prisoners in England and Wales 1970-82: a review of the findings of social research. Joy Mott. 1985. vi + 73pp (0 11 340801 3).

85. Taking account of crime: key findings from the 1984 British Crime Survey. Mike Hough and Pat Mayhew. 1985. vi + 115pp. (0 11 340810 2).

86. Implementing crime prevention measures. Tim Hope. 1985. vi + 82pp. (0 11 340812 9).

87. Resettling refugees: the lessons of research. Simon Field. 1985. vi + 66pp. (0 11 340815 3).

88. Investigating burglary: the measurement of police performance. John Burrows. 1986. v + 36pp. (0 11 340824 2).

ALSO

Designing out crime, R. V. G. Clarke and P. Mayhew (editors). 1980. vii + 186pp. (0 11 340732 7).

(This book collects, with an introduction, studies that were orginally published in HORS 34, 47, 49, 55, 62 and 63 and which are illustrative of the 'situational' approach to crime prevention).

Policing today. Kevin Heal, Roger Tarling and John Burrows (editors). 1985. v + 181pp. (0 11 340800 5).

(This book brings together twelve separate studies on police matters produced during the last few years by the Unit. The collection records some relatively little known contributions to the debate on policing).

The above HMSO publications can be purchased fom Government Bookshops or through booksellers.

The following Home Office research publications are available on request from the Home Office Research and Planning Unit, 50 Queen Anne's Gate, London, SW1H 9AT.

Research Unit Papers (RUP)

1. Uniformed police work and management technology. J. M. Hough. 1980.

2. Supplementary information on sexual offences and sentencing. Roy Walmsley and Karen White. 1980.

3. Board of visitor adjudications. David Smith, Claire Austin and John Ditchfield. 1981.

4. Day centres and probations. Suzan Fairhead, with the assistance of J. Wilkinson-Grey. 1981.

Research and Planning Unit Papers (RPUP)

5. Ethnic minorities and complaints against the police. Philip Stevens and Carole Willis. 1982.

6. *Crime and public housing. Mike Hough and Pat Mayhew (editors). 1982.

7. *Abstracts of race relations research. George Mair and Philip Stevens (editors). 1982.

8. Police probationer training in race relations. Peter Southgate. 1982.

9. *The police response to calls from the public. Paul Ekblom and Kevin Heal. 1982.

10. City centre crime: a situational approach to prevention. Malcolm Ramsay. 1982.

11. Burglary in schools: the prospects for prevention. Tim Hope. 1982.

12. *Fine enforcement. Paul Softley and David Moxon. 1982.

13. Vietnamese refugees. Peter Jones. 1982.

14. Community resources for victims of crime. Karen Williams. 1983.

---

*Out of print

15. The use, effectiveness and impact of police stop and search powers. Carole Willis. 1983.

16. Acquittal rates. Sid Butler. 1983.

17. Criminal justice comparisons: the case of Scotland and England and Wales. Lorna J. F. Smith. 1983.

18. Time taken to deal with juveniles under criminal proceedings. Catherine Frankenburg and Roger Tarling. 1983.

19. Civilian review of complaints against the police: a survey of the United States literature. David C. Brown. 1983.

20. Police action on motoring offences. David Riley. 1983.

21. *Diverting drunks from the criminal justice system. Sue Kingsley and George Mair. 1983.

22. The staff resource implications of an independent prosecution system. Peter R. Jones. 1983.

23. Reducing the prison population: an explanatory study in Hampshire. David Smith, Bill Sheppard, George Mair and Karen Williams. 1984.

24. Criminal justice system model: magistrates' courts' sub-model. Susan Rice. 1984.

25. Measures of police effectiveness and efficiency. Ian Sinclair and Clive Miller. 1984.

26. Punishment practice by prison Boards of Visitors. Susan Iles, Adrienne Connors, Chris May, Joy Mott. 1984.

27. *Reparation, conciliation and mediation. Tony Marshall. 1984.

28. Magistrates domestic courts: new perspectives. Tony Marshall (editor). 1984.

29. Racism awareness training for the police. Peter Southgate. 1984.

30. Community constables: a study of policing initiative. David Brown and Susan Iles. 1985.

31. Recruiting volunteers: Hilary Jackson. 1985.

32. Juvenile sentencing: is there a tariff? David Moxon, Peter Jones and Roger Tarling. 1985.

33. Bringing people together: mediation and reparation projects in Great Britain. Tony Marshall and Martin Walpole. 1985.

34. Rewards in the absence of the accused. Chris May. 1985.

Research Bulletin
The Research Bulleting is published twice a year and consists mainly of short articles relating to projects which are part of the Home Office Research and Planning Unit's research programme.

*Out of print.

Printed for Her Majesty's Stationery Office by   Dd. 739346 C2O. 5/86.